Principles and Practice of Supervisory Management

JOHN MUNRO FRASER MA

Reader in Personnel Management
University of Aston in Birmingham

NELSON

THOMAS NELSON AND SONS LTD
36 Park Street London W1Y 4DE

NELSON (AFRICA) LTD
PO Box 18123 Nairobi Kenya

THOMAS NELSON (AUSTRALIA) LTD
597 Little Collins Street Melbourne 3000

THOMAS NELSON AND SONS (CANADA) LTD
81 Curlew Drive Don Mills Ontario

THOMAS NELSON (NIGERIA) LTD
PO Box 336 Apapa Lagos

ISBN 17 741003 5

Printed in Great Britain by Hazell Watson & Viney Ltd,
Aylesbury, Bucks

Preface

This book has been designed as a text for students taking examinations conducted or approved by the Institute of Supervisory Management or the National Examinations Board in Supervisory Studies. It deals first with organization, Chapter 2 outlining some of the studies which have influenced thinking on this subject and Chapter 3 dealing with the structure of organizations. Chapter 4 gives an account of the duties and responsibilities of the supervisory manager within this structure.

The next part of the book concerns itself with people. Chapter 5 deals with manpower planning and the study of jobs, while Chapter 6 discusses the requirements of these jobs in terms of the personal qualities they call for. Chapter 7 traces the progress of an applicant for employment up to the point where he actually starts on the job. Chapter 8 deals with training and reporting, and discusses the action that must be taken once the report has been made.

Chapter 9 attempts to survey the framework of State regulation within which industry must operate. The final chapter covers the psychological aspects in summary form, in the hope that this may tie some ends together and put this somewhat complex part of the syllabus into perspective.

Having been concerned with supervisory training for a number of years, I am very conscious of the need for a properly controlled standard of qualification of the kind envisaged by the Institute of Supervisory Management and the National Examinations Board in Supervisory Studies. I hope that this little book will play its part in equipping supervisory managers for their very difficult task.

J.M.F.

Contents

9   Legislation   99

The Factories Act, 1961—Shops, Offices, and Railway
Premises Act, 1963—Contracts of Employment Act, 1963
—Redundancy Payments Act, 1965—Disabled Persons
(Employment) Act, 1944—Industrial Training Act, 1964—
Effects of Industrial Legislation—Summary

10 Psychological Aspects   111

Task of Supervisory Manager—Dealing with People—
Organization Structure—Communication—Individual Attitudes—Individual Differences—Day-to-day Work—Understanding Others—Measuring Human Attributes—Conflict
in Industry

Further Reading   117

Index   119

CHAPTER 1 | Introduction

The supervisory manager occupies a key position in any organization. He stands at the point where the plans and policies of those who direct the enterprise are turned into practical results through the efforts of the men and women who work on the job. He is the man who gets things done. And while he may play no direct part in long-term planning, nor actually work on the production process, he must have a firm grasp of both. Without him to bring the two together, our industry would be in a pretty mess. Planning without action achieves nothing. And, while action without planning may achieve something, the results are seldom worth either the time or the effort.

The first thing the modern supervisory manager needs to know is where he stands in the organization. This calls for some understanding of the structure of a modern industrial or commercial enterprise. Modern industry or commerce, however, presents a many-sided picture, and it is very easy to give an over-simplified view. Trade unions are claiming an increasing say in what goes on, while the State is extending its control. The techniques of production have an influence on the working of any organization, while, in the final analysis, industry or commerce is an economic venture. The man who holds the purse strings always exercises a very large measure of control. To think of an industrial firm as a simple unified structure, answerable solely to the direction of the man at the top, is to fail to understand present-day realities.

Problems of Present-day Organization

Any organization must have a certain inner strength if it is to survive. It cannot simply become a battleground where shop stewards and rate fixers, cost accountants and progress chasers, factory inspectors and the Inland Revenue wage guerilla war. Sectional interests, however legitimate they may be, cannot take over control. There must be a central core of responsibility and authority, running from the chief executive to the floor of the shop and back again. This is the 'central nervous system' of the organization. And it must be the quickest means of communication within it. Information must pass inwards along it more effectively than by any other means. Plans for action must pass outwards along it, so that the right thing gets done at the right time in the right place. One of the dangers we face today is the slowing down of this central nervous system. When anaesthesia attacks the sensory nerves, and paralysis affects the motor nerves, then the risk of anarchy is not far away. No one at the top knows what is happening on the factory floor, while the people on the job couldn't care less what the front office is on about.

In the past, organizations have been able to support their authority by disciplinary sanctions. The Armed Forces could put their lower ranks 'on a charge' and apply punishments of increasing severity. In industry or commerce, sanctions were less conventionalized, but they were none the less severe. An employee could be deprived of his livelihood and forced to join the ranks of the unemployed, living on a minimum subsistence standard with little prospect of another job. Even with trade-union representation, this left a very real power in the hands of management—power which was not always linked with responsibility at the lower levels. Up to the Second World War, there were few personnel problems that couldn't be solved by sacking someone. This provided an authoritarian background to management, of which people were not always consciously aware. It enabled those in charge of an organization to close their eyes to the fact that they had brought a large number of people together to work for several hours in the day in pursuit of the organization's objectives. They could disregard the fact that these people remained human beings, not simply units in a production process.

The appearance of full employment, for the first time in human history, has cut the ground from under the feet of the authoritarian organization. Employees can now rely on a degree of protection far beyond the dreams of Factory Acts, redundancy payments, or collective bargaining agreements. They can pick and choose among jobs; they can bring a highly integrated production system to a stop by a walkout in a small department; they can make nonsense of the rate of overhead recovery by a slowdown or an overtime ban. The 'take it or leave it' style of management is now completely helpless. It can be pushed about at will by the factory floor. And only a fundamental change of attitude will ever enable it to regain any sort of control over what goes on in its own factory.

Importance of the Supervisory Manager

To meet this situation several steps will be necessary. The first of these concerns the structure of organization. This must be coherent from top to bottom, so that everyone knows where he stands. At each level, there must be a stable and reliable relationship with the next level above and the next one below. This is particularly important at the supervisory level, for this is where the most serious weaknesses can be found in most existing organizations.

As has been said, the supervisory manager stands between planning and action. If he is not in the confidence of the planners, there will be no effective action. Similarly, if those on whose muscles the action depends cannot rely on him as their link with the planners, the factory floor will begin to organize itself. And this organization will not be in line with that of management, nor will it have the same ends in view. The position of the supervisory manager in the structure is therefore of the first importance. He himself must be clear about it. Those above him must respect it and give him the support he needs. Those below must find him their most reliable link with the rest of the organization.

This central core of an organization must have a certain toughness of fibre if it is to hold the structure together. As has been pointed out, we can no longer think in terms of a simple unified structure, relying on authoritarian discipline to make it work. Different interests now claim legitimate representation, and have methods of supporting their claims. But if the responses of this central nervous system are sufficiently rapid and effective, it can adapt to these pressures and still retain control. If these responses are too slow, control will slip out of the hands of management and the risk of anarchy will be just around the corner.

People at Work

Next we have the problem of maintaining control in a non-authoritarian situation. In the past, people have talked a great deal about leadership but have overlooked the fact that most of our leader figures have been backed up by a system of effective sanctions. However impressive their personal qualities may have been, they could usually make it decidedly unpleasant one way or another for those who did not respond to their direction. Factory-floor leadership in present-day industry, however, makes a much heavier demand than crisis leadership at one of the dramatic moments in history. It calls for different, and perhaps harder-wearing, personal qualities. Among these must be a deeper understanding of human beings, their aims and aspirations, and their reactions to pressure. This understanding must be in terms of the day-by-day realities of working life, and not in abstruse psychological theorizing. It must give practical guidance on the routine supervision of personnel, as well as encouraging some insight into why people do things.

Human beings are complex entities, perhaps the most complex

we shall ever encounter. They are capable of surprising amounts of effort, but the conditions under which they will produce these efforts are difficult to understand. In industry or commerce, people work for money in the shape of their wages or salaries. How hard they will work for a given amount of money, however, cannot always be accurately predicted. If it could, many of our supervisory management problems would be solved. But people differ from one to the next, and their motivation differs also. Other conditions play a part in the amount of effort they will put forth in a given situation. Many of these conditions depend on the relationships and expectations among the other human beings around them. Success in supervisory management often depends on insight into these delicate and intangible issues—insight which does not always come easily to the down-to-earth, practical man.

Demands of the State

Work is part of daily life in the community. It can no longer be kept apart and allowed to run itself according to a set of private rules. The conditions under which our fellow citizens earn their living are now governed by State regulations. These attempt to maintain standards acceptable to the national conscience, in contrast to what was permitted in the early beginnings of our industry. Management is no longer king in its own castle. It is answerable to the community as a whole through various Acts of Parliament. Every manager must not only be familiar with these Acts, he must adapt his thinking to the intentions behind them. He must also anticipate the next stage ahead. Merely minimal compliance with the rules of today usually means being caught with one's pants down by the rules of tomorrow.

No one can be successful in present-day management if his mental horizon is bounded by the factory or office wall. Changes are taking place in our way of life, and the rate of change is itself speeding up. This applies not only to technical processes, materials, and products; it applies also to the place of industry and commerce in our life as a nation. Two world wars made it necessary for industry to be adapted to the needs of a national emergency. The framework of control which this brought into being has made possible a degree of regulation which had not previously been practicable. Industry and commerce can now be harnessed to the needs of the community, not only in productive and financial terms, but also in terms of the way of life it provides for those engaged in it. We no longer accept large-scale unemployment and its associated poverty as inevitable. We now take for granted standards of living and self-respect undreamed of 30 years ago. Unless the supervisory manager is aware of these expectations, he will find difficulty in adapting to a changing way of life.

Final Considerations

Supervisory management is the management of men and women at work in the situation of the present day. It is an aspect of management which is of increasing importance as our way of life develops. 'Human relations' is a term which has fallen momentarily into disrepute. It is thought to smell of paternalism, do-goodism, and the failure to face up to the inevitability of conflict in industry and commerce. Nevertheless, this is the aspect of management in which we are furthest behind at the moment. Whether we call it organizational behaviour, industrial sociology, or man management, it is the aspect which holds promise of greatest progress, if we can only deepen our understanding of its implications. Higher standards of living are one result of expanding industrialization. Higher standards of self-respect and fulfilment as individuals are also within our grasp.

CHAPTER 2 | **Industrial Organization**

Whenever more than one person is working on a job, some form of organization is necessary. Each must know which part is his responsibility and what standards he is expected to achieve. Each must understand how his task fits in with what the others are doing. There must be someone who checks his work. There must be someone to whom he can turn when anything goes wrong. And there must be someone who takes responsibility for getting the whole job completed.

When we say that an enterprise has been properly organized, this is what we mean. Tasks have been laid out so that each fits logically with the next. Each person knows exactly what he has to do and how his work will be checked. Each person has been adequately instructed and trained. Each has been provided with the tools, material, and equipment that he needs to do his job. Each person knows who is in charge and has confidence in his ability to help out in any doubt or difficulty that may crop up in the work.

But while we know what organization is meant to achieve, it is not always clear how we should set about it. The end result may be obvious enough. In any industrial or commercial organization, for example, the end result is the production of goods or services. And if the enterprise is to survive, all the factors in production—men, materials, and equipment—must be used efficiently and economically. But the means towards this end may be difficult and complex, involving expensive plant and buildings, intricate technological processes, and hundreds of highly trained personnel. Providing these means of production may require large outlays of capital. And making them work together effectively in practice will present a number of formidable problems.

Theories of Organization
It may help if we have a set of principles to guide us. The first person who tried to provide these was a German, Max Weber. He laid down that effective organization depends upon the following:

1 *Fixed areas of responsibility*, within which the duties of individuals are specified, and their powers and authority strictly defined.
2 *Properly trained and qualified people*, who can fulfil the duties required of them, to take charge of each of these areas.

3 *Graded levels of authority*, which allow ordered supervision of lower officials by those above. These also provide for a regulated system of appeals.

4 *General rules which are consistent and stable*, governing the duties attached to each office. Each official must be trained in these, and must regulate his decisions in accordance with them.

5 *Written documents, office space, and necessary equipment*, available to all qualified officials. These are not their personal property, but belong to the position. Like all his other activities during working hours, they must be kept separate from the official's private life and interests.

Weber gave the name *bureaucracy* to this theory of organization. And, while things have moved forward since he wrote nearly 50 years ago, he still deserves attention. He was the first to set out a consistent set of principles, and these principles still hold good. It may be easy to criticize a bureaucratic organization for its rigidity and lack of flexibility. We may condemn the petty bureaucrat for his insistence on sticking to the rules and his failure to recognize a special case. But unless an organization is based on principles which have something in common with those above, it won't last long. Enthusiasm and personal loyalty have their place in any organization, but in the long term people have got to know where they stand. And inspired leadership will never replace careful attention to detail.

Beginnings of Industrial Organization

Industry did not begin in any organized fashion. In its present form, it goes back less than 200 years. It has no history and no literature, for it has never attracted the attention of great authors or thinkers. It has few great names, for those who sought a place in history more often found it in politics, government, or war. Industry grew up by itself, from the grass roots. It was hardly noticed by the people who governed the country. In fact, at one stage, there was a theory that government should leave industry alone. If everyone was allowed to pursue his own advantage without interference, it was argued, the greatest good for the greatest number would result. This *laissez-faire* philosophy was widely accepted in the beginning of the nineteenth century.

Modern industry has grown up partly through the initiative of individuals and partly through the development of technical processes. Spinning and weaving, which had always been done in the cottages, were transformed by the invention of mechanical processes which speeded them up. When the steam engine was invented, banks of machines could be driven from the same source of power. Thus the factory became possible, in which a number of people worked together for several hours in the day. This presented the first big problem of industrial organization. It was not recognized as such, however, for the people in charge were only concerned with the technical, commercial, and financial developments. They thought that the human or organizational sides could be left to look after themselves. We are only now realizing how wrong they were.

When people began to work together in large numbers, a form of organization grew up by itself from the bottom. In some cases, this was a pretty tough one, centring on the authority of the foreman. In the nineteenth century the employer had almost unlimited power over his employees. He could sack them at will, thus depriving them of their livelihood and reducing them to the miserable conditions of the poorhouse. There were no effective trade unions, so they lacked the protection of collective action. These powers were delegated to the foreman who used them as he thought fit. No one else worried much, so long as he got the work done. The factory owner wasn't concerned, provided he got results. What the workers felt about it didn't worry anyone either. They had no means of presenting their grievances. And, if they didn't like it, there were plenty more waiting at the gate. So, if they had any sense, they kept their mouths shut and put up with it. All this gave the foreman enormous power over the workers under him—power which we find difficult to understand today.

But the on-the-job organization sometimes worked in another way. The navvies who built the railways usually worked in gangs, on a price per ton for the amount of earth shifted. These gangs were largely self-organized, and they were often self-selected. That is to say, a newcomer could be taken into the gang if the other members accepted him, and he could stay as long as he fitted into the group's way of working. Miners worked under butty contractors, who bargained with the mine owner to extract the coal. Piece payments were widespread in the early days, and gangers were often in the position of sub-contractors.

From our point of view, these small, face-to-face working groups are important. In the first place, they were not fully integrated into the organization. They ran themselves according to their own rules. Tasks were shared out by mutual agreement, and working methods were haphazard and traditional. Standards of output were determined by the group itself, and the only contact with the larger organization was through a wage bargain or a piecework price. No one outside the group had any authority over the individual members. And leadership of the group depended on acceptance by the others, rather than on formal appointment.

When we think of industry in these terms, it is obvious that it was not organized in the sense outlined in the preceding section. Areas of responsibility were not defined, nor were people put in charge of them who had been properly trained for their positions. Levels of authority were vague and indefinite, and there were no general rules to govern the duties attached to each office. This sort of informal grass-roots organization may have produced results in the conditions of the nineteenth and early twentieth centuries. But these results were not as good as they might have been in terms of economical working. And they were achieved at the cost of a great deal of human suffering.

F. W. Taylor and Scientific Management

The first person to realize these inefficiencies was an American, Frederick Winslow Taylor, 'the father of scientific management'. As a supervisor in an engineering firm in the 1880s, he began to study the methods of work. He found that, by systematic observation and experiment, they could be made much more efficient. In fact, he reckoned that some operators could reach at least twice their existing levels of output, if they used the methods he devised.

When he tried to introduce these methods, however, he met determined resistance from the factory floor. Operators insisted that the standards he set were impossible, and they refused even to try to meet them. When he timed their work in detail and supervised them from moment to moment, they sabotaged their machines to prove that they were being run too hard. New starters trained by Taylor himself were intimidated by the others if they tried to achieve the levels of output he set. If Taylor had not been a quite exceptional person he would have given up in disgust. As it was, he continued in the face of this determined opposition, and succeeded in raising the standards of output, in some cases to twice their former level. But this was at the price of a great deal of conflict and ill-feeling. And it was at a time when heavy unemployment and the lack of any trade union organization made it possible to sack workers at a moment's notice.

Thinking over what had happened, Taylor concluded that there was something badly wrong with the methods of management.

According to him, these depended solely on initiative and incentive. Management contented itself with offering an incentive in the form of a wage or a piecework price. It left the workers to use their initiative to earn their money in the way they thought best. This, in fact, is the fault in the kind of early industrial organization described above. It stops short of the point where the work is actually done. And it leaves too much to be sorted out by the people on the job.

Taylor felt that management was shirking its responsibilities. He thought that it ought to take more interest in the workers' jobs and their methods of work. He summed up his views in the following four principles of what he called scientific management:

1 Management ought to work out an *efficient method* for each worker's job.
2 Management ought to *select* suitable workers for each job and *train* them in these methods.
3 Management ought to *ensure* that all jobs are *actually done* in accordance with the methods and standards they have developed.
4 Management ought to *accept responsibility* for all planning and organization, instead of leaving it to the workers.

Taylor applied these principles when he was with the Bethlehem Steel Co., with considerable success. The best-known example is his pig-iron handling study where the average daily tonnage loaded was $12\frac{1}{2}$ per man. By studying the job and supervising an operator from moment to moment throughout the day, he got him to load $47\frac{1}{2}$ tons. Taylor and his assistants had taken over the responsibility for the methods and standards on the job, and thus had nearly quadrupled the output.

Better-planned organization and properly studied methods of work can improve output. But they are not the whole story. They leave out the human factor during working hours. And this can make itself felt in some unexpected ways. People are not machines which can be switched on and off like an electric motor. They bring their personal feelings, their opinions and attitudes, their awkwardnesses and their little ways with them to work in the morning. And unless someone takes account of these, they will get in the way of the organization's activities.

This is the criticism that can be levelled against what we have said up to now. We have been taking a *mechanistic* view of organization at work. We have been thinking in terms of a fixed and inflexible structure. And we have been putting individuals into positions like pegs into slots. This tends to reduce them to units in a framework, or factors in the productive or distributive process. From Taylor onwards, this approach spread widely throughout management thinking. Many consultants studied methods of work and organization, and produced dramatic results in increased efficiency. Studies were also made of the physical conditions of work, and changes were made which further increased output.

But under it all was an attitude towards the worker that was something less than human. Taylor studied him in terms of the weights he could lift and the distance he could walk without fatigue. Frank Gilbreth timed him on each element of the job and trained him in the most efficient methods. Others encouraged him to work harder by various payment-by-results schemes, and kept him up to scratch by the threat of losing his high earnings. But no one allowed him to be a human being with any feelings of his own during working hours. Nor could he have any sense of identification with other people, or any relationships with them outside the formal channels of the organization. We have a kind of nightmare picture of a crowd of robots working silently and mechanically at their tasks, with blank minds and set faces, thinking of nothing except the money they are earning, until the whistle blows.

Hawthorne Studies

It is always a mistake to believe that human beings can be treated as isolated individuals, or that they can put large areas of their personality into cold storage during working hours. This is where the face-to-face group on the job can come into collision with the formal organization. In the former, a chap can be a human being, liked and respected by other human beings, working with them on a common task. The small group can command loyalty and a sense of identification. When it is properly integrated into the larger organization, it can call out a considerable degree of extra effort from its members. When it cuts across the larger organization, on the other hand, it can influence the members into restricting output and otherwise setting themselves against its aims and purposes.

This was illustrated by a series of studies carried out in the Hawthorne Works of the Western Electric Co., near Chicago, in the 1920s. These began in an attempt to find out the effect of better lighting on the operators' output. Bulbs were changed to those of higher power, and each change resulted in an improvement in efficiency. But when further changes to bulbs of lower power still produced higher output, it became clear that other factors were at work. The mechanistic approach that better working conditions were directly associated with higher efficiency proved not to be the whole story. There must be some other factor in the situation. The problem was to find what that factor could be.

The next attempt started with six girls who were put into a room by themselves. They worked on a repetitive task on the assembly of telephone relays (the Relay Assembly Test Room). Changes were made in the hours of work, and rest pauses were introduced at different periods in the day. With each change, output went up, linking up with the idea that better conditions resulted in increased efficiency. What shook the experimenters was the fact that when the rest pauses were withdrawn and the hours put back to their original length, output reached its highest level ever. It was once more obvious that none of the physical changes had been the real cause of the improvement. The essential factor had escaped again. What could it have been?

After several years of observation, it was finally concluded that the missing factor had been the formation of a small group, integrated with the rest of the organization. The girls had become friendly together. They had talked and gossiped throughout the day, had taken an interest in each other, and had celebrated each others' birthdays and similar events. They had got on well with the supervisor who was, in fact, a research worker interested in the experiment for its own sake. The girls had come to depend on him and had worked as a group under his guidance. As a result the group had identified itself with the purpose of the organization. It had called out more effort from the individual members, and had given them a reward in day-to-day friendship and individual significance during working hours.

An entirely opposite result was found in the Bank Wiring Room study. This consisted of fourteen men engaged on the wiring and soldering of telephone switchboards. But here the groupings which gave the individuals their sense of belonging and identification were antagonistic to the larger organization. To remain 'one of the boys' in these informal face-to-face groups, the worker had to limit his output and not show himself too friendly with the supervisor. If he worked too hard, the group expressed its disapproval in various ways. And if the supervisor tried to throw his weight around too much, he was told to go and chase himself. Effective control on the job was exercised by the informal group, not by the representative of the formal organization.

The Hawthorne Studies fill an important gap in our understanding of organization at work. They show that this human factor can work either for or against its purpose. If the role we expect of a human being during working hours is a satisfying and self-respecting one, several things will follow. He will identify himself with it, and apply his effort to the task et for him. He will form satisfying relationships with those around him, and play his part in the official groupings. But if we neglect this element in the work situation, it will escape our control. If we try to treat human beings as isolated individuals, they will form unofficial relationships in informal groupings. And if the roles we offer them are neither satisfying nor self-respecting, they will find roles in these unofficial groups which meet their needs to belong and be appreciated. Thus, no matter how carefully we define the responsibilities, study the tasks, work out the methods, and train the operators, this human factor can escape our control if we do not recognize it. The basic problem is to ensure that the groups within which people form relationships during working hours are integrated into the larger organization. Only then can the purpose of the organization be appreciated and accepted by those who work in it.

Supervisory Management

How does all this affect the job of the supervisory manager? Well, it should provide some framework within which we can arrange our ideas. This will fall into the following main divisions.

Operational responsibility. The supervisor has been entrusted with a fixed area of responsibility within the larger organization. He must start by knowing exactly what he is responsible for, and the standards on which he will be judged. Obviously this will lead into quite a lot of detail when we consider a particular job. In general terms, however, there will be standards of output and quality. There will be budgets for direct costs—material, labour, and anything actually used on the job—and also for overhead recovery or the allocation of indirect costs. There will be questions of maintenance, labour relations, safety, and the like, which we shall go into later. The essential point at this stage is that he should know exactly what his duties are, and what results he is expected to achieve.

His area of responsibility will be within a series of graded levels of authority. The supervisory manager should know whom he is responsible to. This sounds simple, but in a larger organization it can raise complications. He will have an immediate boss to whom he reports on the overall running of his section. But there will also be specialists who are concerned with different aspects of his job. There may be an inspector who is responsible for standards of quality. There may be a production controller who sets his programme of work. There may be others also with whom we shall deal later on. The point at this moment is that he should know where he stands with each of these people; what services he can expect of them; and what they will expect of him.

There will also be general rules or policies which will govern the various decisions he has to make. The supervisory manager must know how the organization expects him to deal with various situations as they arise. Whenever he makes an on-the-spot decision, he should not simply be thinking about how to overcome that particular crisis. He should be applying the organization's policy as it affects that situation. In this way his decisions will be consistent—and not only with each other: they will fit in with all the decisions that are being made by other supervisory managers when they are faced with a similar situation.

Technical responsibility. Within his area of responsibility, the supervisory manager must ensure that standards of efficient working are maintained. This will start with the actual methods used on each job. Either on his own, or with the collaboration of a work study department, he must make certain that neither time nor effort is wasted. For each task, there should be a method worked out that makes best use of the operator's time. New operators must be suitable for these tasks and have the skills or aptitudes required. Once selected, they must be trained in the methods until they can reach the standards of output expected.

Once he knows what can be reasonably expected of trained operators, he must face the next problem. This is to ensure that the proper methods are actually being used on the job, and that the standards of output are being achieved. He need not spend all day and every day breathing down the necks of the people under his charge. But he must be certain that none of them is getting away with less than can be reasonably expected of him during working hours, and that none of them is managing to look busy and occupied, while in fact he is producing less than the standard output.

Once again, the details here will depend on the actual job, and cannot be discussed except in general terms. Once a supervisory manager has grasped certain principles, however, he should be able quickly to determine whether a job is being done efficiently or otherwise. Systematic work study has made considerable progress in recent years. And once the essentials have been understood, it is not difficult to see when effort is being properly applied, and when time is being wasted by unnecessary movements or badly placed equipment.

Personnel responsibility. The third aspect of supervisory management concerns the people within his area of responsibility. This is the aspect which perhaps presents the greatest challenge. It is the one on which success or failure most directly depends, and it is the one which calls his own personal qualities into play on the job. If a supervisory manager can cope successfully with the problems which this aspect presents, he can make his most important contribution to present-day industry.

It is the supervisory manager's job to see that the people under him are working as a team. He is the only one who can do this, as he is the person in direct contact with them. He must ensure that the groups they fall into are integrated into the organization. He must also ensure that there is a proper understanding of the purposes of the organization, and that these purposes are accepted, so that effort is applied towards their fulfilment. This involves knowing his people as individuals and appreciating their skills and capabilities. The supervisory manager must know who is friendly with whom, and how they get on together. He must make sure that no groups form which are at odds with the organization, and that no influence is exerted which cuts across the formal lines.

We must never forget that the supervisor is primarily there to manage people. Machines and processes come second, and the problems they present are practical ones. There is always a solution to a practical problem. It may take a little time and some specialized knowledge to find it, but the answer is always there. There is not always an answer to the problems presented by people. Sometimes we have to live with these for a long time, and the best we can do is simply to tide them over. But they present the most important part of the supervisory manager's job, and if he can cope with this, the other parts will fall into place.

SUMMARY

1 *What is Max Weber's theory of bureaucracy?*

This lays down that effective organization must be based on the following principles:

(a) *Fixed areas of responsibility*, each under the charge of a *properly qualified person*.

  (b) *Graded levels of authority* to allow for ordered supervision of lower officials by those above. This also provides for a system of appeals.
  (c) *General rules*, embodied in written documents available to all officials, which provide a stable and consistent framework within which to carry out their duties.

The importance of these principles is that they form the first attempt at setting out a theory of organization.

2 *How did industrial organization begin?*

Usually in the form of small, self-organized groups, operating on a piecework rate or a money bargain with the owners of the business. These groups were not integrated into a larger organization, nor did they follow any general rules, as set out above. Each group operated, officially or unofficially, on a kind of sub-contracting basis. The only exceptions to this were where the immediate foreman could exercise unrestricted disciplinary powers.

3 *What is the significance of F. W. Taylor's work?*

Taylor was the first to study the working methods of these factory-floor groupings in detail. He found that they were less efficient than they might be, and that there was an unofficial code of restriction on output. He laid the responsibility for this at the door of management, and set out the principles on which *scientific management* should be based. These are:

  (a) Management is responsible for working out an *efficient method* for each job in the factory.
  (b) Management should *select and train* operators in the methods it has worked out.
  (c) Management should ensure that the jobs are being done *in accordance with these methods.*
  (d) Management is responsible for the *planning and organization* of everything that goes on during working hours. It should not leave this to the operators.

4 *What do we mean by a 'mechanistic' approach to organization?*

The *mechanistic* approach leads one to think of organization as a fixed and inflexible structure. It tends also to make one deal with people as units, or factors in the production process. Taylor's approach to the operator, for example, was as a sensory-motor organism actuated solely by a desire to earn money. This tends to leave out the human factor, which can upset the working of a perfect organization when it is neglected. The organic approach, in which the organization is regarded as a living entity, is more realistic.

5 *What is the significance of the Hawthorne Studies?*

They called attention to this neglected human factor. They consisted of the following stages:

(a) *Experiments in lighting* which showed that improved lighting did not by itself affect productivity.
(b) *The Relay Assembly Test Room* which showed that improved relations among a group of operators had more effect on productivity than changes in hours or rest pauses.
(c) *The Bank Wiring Room* study which called attention to the unofficial, anti-management groupings within the official management organization.

6 *What light does all this throw on the job of the supervisory manager?*

(a) He is in charge of a fixed area of responsibility, within a framework of organization which consists of graded levels of authority, and works to stable and consistent general rules.
(b) Within this area of responsibility he ensures that the necessary tasks are done by efficient methods and that full use is made of the men, materials, and machines under his charge.
(c) He is responsible for the people within his area of responsibility, and must ensure that they work as a team to achieve their part of the objectives of the organization.

In considering organization, the first point we must be clear about is its structure. This must be logical and coherent, so that the various parts fit properly together. Without an adequate structure, communication within the organization will be unsatisfactory. And without effective communication, control will be impossible.

Line Organization

The first and simplest aspect of this structure is the line organization. This shows the various levels as they go downwards from higher management to the operators on the job. At each level, the person in charge is answerable to the one above him. The line organization, in fact, shows the graded levels of authority which we discussed in the

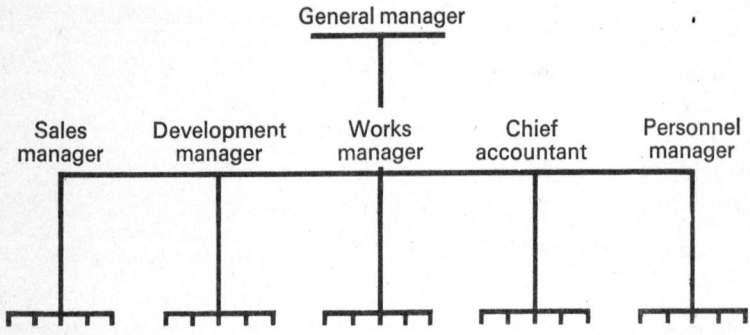

FIG. 1. *T-chart of top management organization*

previous chapter. It also shows the fixed areas of responsibility which make up the structure.

The conventional way of showing the line organization is by the T-chart. One of these is illustrated in Fig. 1. This shows the higher and middle management organization of a typical industrial company. The general manager, or chief executive, is responsible for its overall working. Under him are managers in charge of sales, development, works (or production), finance (or accounts), and personnel. Each of these, in turn, has his own subordinates. These lines on the chart take the shape of a series of capital Ts—hence the name. T-charts are useful for laying down lines of direct responsibility. At the upper levels of an organization, they can be quite simple and straightforward.

T-charts, however, have their limitations. They tend to get more complex as we go farther down the organizational ladder. They take up a lot of space, if we want to get everything in. More seriously, perhaps, they do not give any idea of the cross-links in an organization. Nor do they show the interpersonal relationships between the people at the various levels. These relationships are very important, for unless the officials at each level are in close touch with each other and are in each other's confidence, the organization will not work

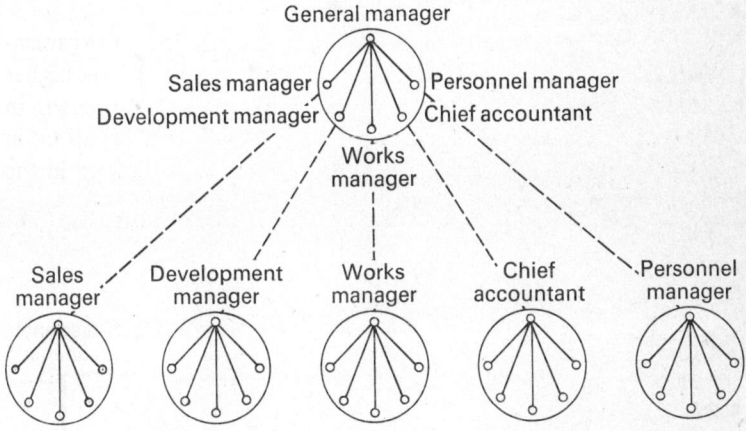

Fig. 2. *Interlocking group chart showing the same organization*

effectively. Organizations depend upon communication. And communication takes place between people. Unless these people are on the right terms with each other, blockages and misunderstandings will arise.

At each level on the chart, therefore, there should be continuous interchange between the manager and his subordinates. There should also be interchanges between the subordinates themselves. These should draw them into a sort of pattern of relationships centring on the manager in charge. Each level, therefore, should form a grouping. And these groupings, in fact, make up the structure of the organization. At the lower levels, operators may be working all day and every day in the same grouping. And their satisfaction in the job may depend to a great extent on whether the relationships in that group are good-humoured and happy. At the higher levels, these groups will not be continuously together. They may meet only occasionally, and the managers concerned will find themselves involved in other patterns of relationships. There will still be interchange between the members, however. And unless the quality of these relationships is reasonably good, things will go wrong in the organization.

Fig. 2 shows the same organization drawn out so as to emphasize the patterns of relationship which must exist between these managers. The general manager has been shown at the centre of a pattern made

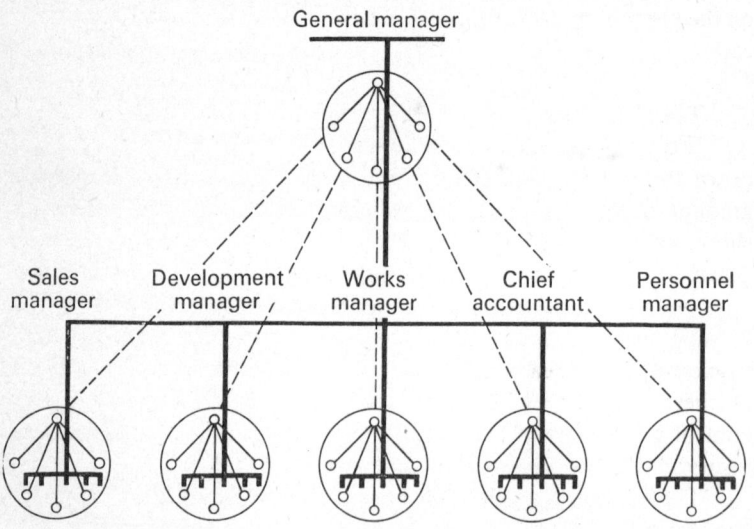

Fig. 3. *Interlocking group chart superimposed on T-chart*

up of his immediate subordinates. This has been enclosed in a circle to emphasize the close relationships which should exist between them.

Each of these managers, however, has his own group of subordinates. These are shown in the circles below, where the middle managers appear at the centre of the patterns. Similarly close relationships should exist within these circles. It will be noticed that the middle managers appear twice in this diagram, once as subordinate members of the top group, and again as central figures in the groups below. This brings out the fact that they form the link between them. They do not, however, act merely as post offices, carrying messages from one to the other. They have a constructive role to play in each. In the upper group, they must support the general manager. In the lower groups, they must interpret the policies decided upon in the top group, and make the decisions required of them by their subordinates.

Fig. 3 shows the interlocking group chart superimposed on the T-chart. This helps to illustrate the relationships between the members at this level of the organization, while at the same time it brings out the lines of communication and control. It may look rather complicated at first glance, but it is worth a little study, for it reveals the close terms which these people should be on with each other. If each of the groups shown in the circle is working as a team; and if these teams are linked together by twin subordinate-leadership roles on the part of the members; then there will be a free flow of communication, decision making, and control throughout the organization.

The Shop Floor

We can—indeed we should—carry an organization chart right down to the floor of the shop. Problems arise, however, about the amount of detail that can be included at the lower levels. Fig. 4 shows such a chart, but only one line has been carried all the way down. To make it cover all the subordinates of each manager would have needed a sheet 125 times as wide. This would add up to about 25 yards of paper. Many organization charts, therefore, become a bit vague when they reach the lower levels. This is unfortunate, for it is at these lower levels that the most difficult communication and control problems can arise. And it is at these levels that the supervisory manager's area of responsibility will be found.

The interlocking group chart superimposed on the T-chart in Fig. 4 shows groups of six people at each level. In other words, each official has a *span of control* of five subordinates. This is sometimes put forward as a maximum number at the higher levels. It is felt that with more than this, the close relationships which are essential to effective working become difficult or impossible. At the lower levels, however, supervisory managers are often found with larger numbers under their direct charge. This raises an important point about the structure of an organization. Should there be a maximum number of subordinates for each manager? And should the same maximum be enforced right down to the shop floor? Two difficult problems are involved here.

On the one hand, if we insist on a maximum of five subordinates, the number of levels will tend to increase. Communication difficulties may thus build up with the added number of steps in the line. On the other hand, if we leave the supervisor with too many subordinates, he will not be able to keep in touch with them all. Thus, another source of communication breakdown may arise. This is a problem of considerable importance at the lower levels. It sounds

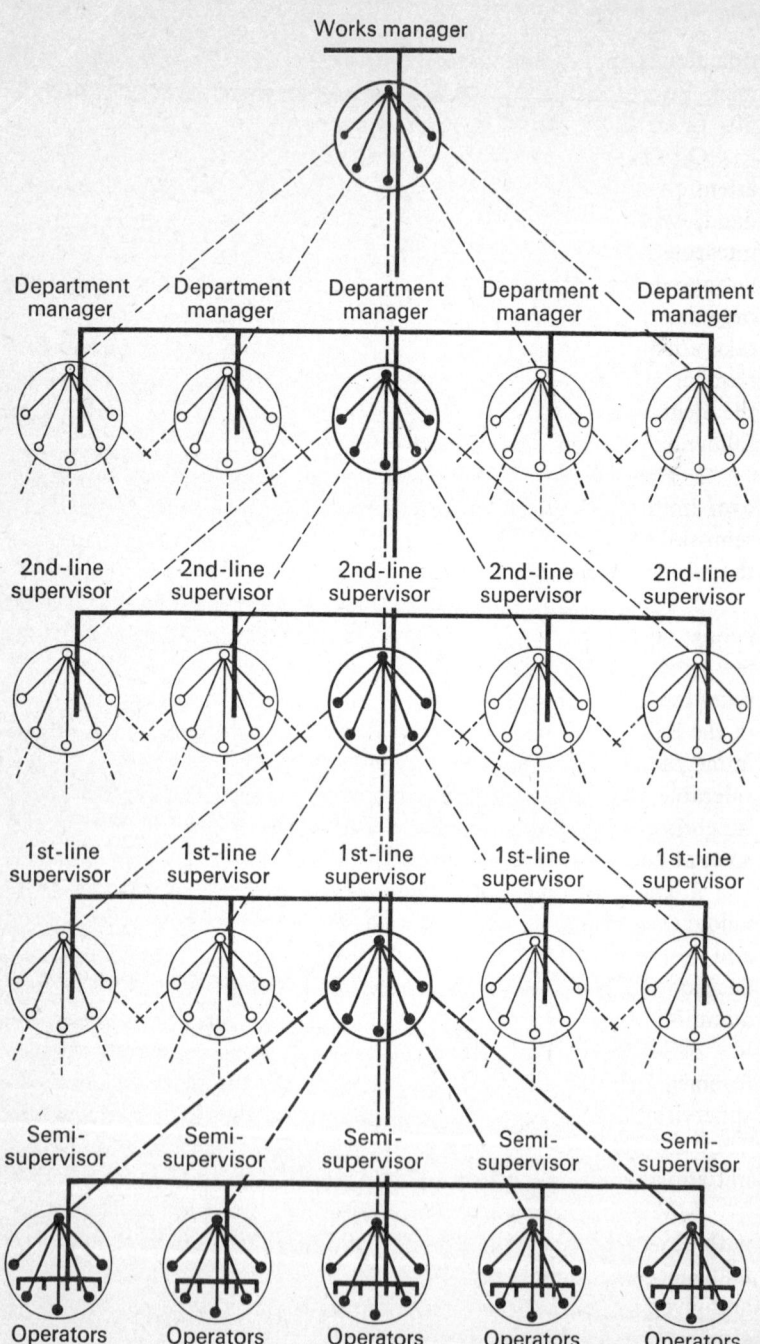

FIG. 4. *Organization chart showing line organization*

ridiculous to lay down that there should be a supervisor to every five men. But, on the other hand, if we expect a supervisor to control fifty or sixty, we are setting him an impossible task.

Organization structure on the factory floor has not had the attention it deserves. The Hawthorne Studies showed, on the one hand, what could be gained by having a small group properly integrated into the organization. They also showed what can go wrong when unofficial groups grow up which cut across the formal organization. Can an organization's structure be adapted so as to take advantage of these findings? One approach is to consider the number of levels of authority which come into being, and to think of the degree of responsibility that can be expected of each. The following list has emerged from some studies on these lines.

1 The operator. This is the individual who is responsible for his own immediate task and nothing more. He may be highly skilled, semi-skilled, or even unskilled. But he has little concern outside the job which has been allocated to him.

2 The semi-supervisor. In most organizations, however, we find people doing an operator's job who have a little responsibility for a few others around them. Machine-tool setters, service hands, and relief hands are examples of these. They play a very important part in the day-to-day working, for they form the central figures in the immediate working groups on the job, and they can exercise a considerable influence within them. Once the importance of the semi-supervisor has been recognized, we are well on the way to solving the span-of-control problem at the lower levels.

3 The first-line supervisor. This is the first level where the individual does not do an operator's job. He is full-time on supervision, and his responsibility is for the work of other people. Planning, decision making, and communication take up all his time and attention.

4 Second- and third-line supervisors. Sometimes we find general foremen or superintendents at the next stage above the first-line supervisor. Their tasks are similar, but may cover a wider range. They are still interpreting rules and policies, however, rather than initiating new developments.

5 Middle management. At this level, we become less concerned with day-to-day routine, and more with new developments. A middle manager has usually been put in charge of a certain area of activity and given some liberty of action in how he sets about his task. He is also being judged on results, so that his area of decision making is rather wider.

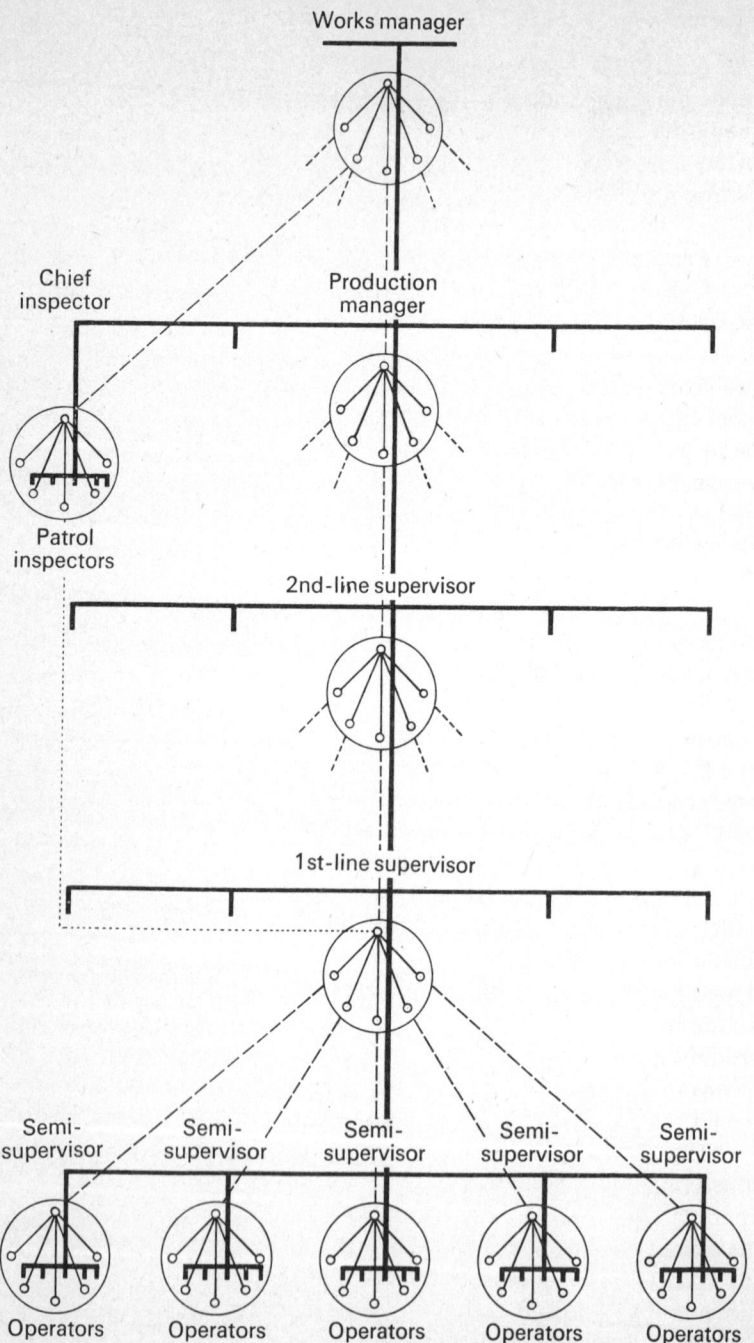

FIG. 5. *Chart showing functional link with inspection department*

6 Higher management. At this level we are concerned with long-range planning, with the setting of objectives, and the provision of the resources necessary to achieve them. The job has become more of an intellectual exercise. The actual down-to-earth problems of getting production out belong in the lower levels.

Functional or Specialist Departments

Over and above the line organization, most firms have specialist departments. To understand these, it helps if we think for a moment about how they come into existence. Suppose a company has a problem about the quality of its products—for example, if complaints from customers begin to pile up. The obvious thing to do then would be to pick out a likely man and tell him to find out what is going wrong. He would examine the faulty products, and would probably find that certain types of defect were cropping up in most of them. He would then report that checks should be carried out, so that these defects could be spotted and corrected at various stages in the production process. 'All right,' says the management, 'we'll appoint inspectors for each of these stages. You show them what to look for, and take charge of them on the job.'

By now the company has got itself an inspection or quality control department. This has its own boss—the chief inspector—and its own staff—the patrol inspectors attached to each stage in the production process. But how do all these fit into the line organization? The chief inspector can be made responsible to the works manager. And his patrol inspectors will form a group of subordinates around him. But what about these patrol inspectors and their link-up with the line supervisors of the production departments? This touches off the real problem of the functional or specialist departments in day-to-day working. If the patrol inspectors butt in on the supervisor's area of responsibility, they can interfere with his authority and arouse his resentment. On the other hand, if they do not insist on having their say about the quality of the products, they are not doing the job for which they were appointed.

The answer, of course, is intelligent collaboration between the supervisory manager and the functional specialist. Each must appreciate the other's responsibility. The specialist must realize that the overall running of the section rests with the supervisor, while the supervisor must understand what the specialist is there for. He must give him the facilities he needs, and make effective use of the services he offers. Fig. 5 shows in diagrammatic form how a specialist inspection department would be integrated into the line organization

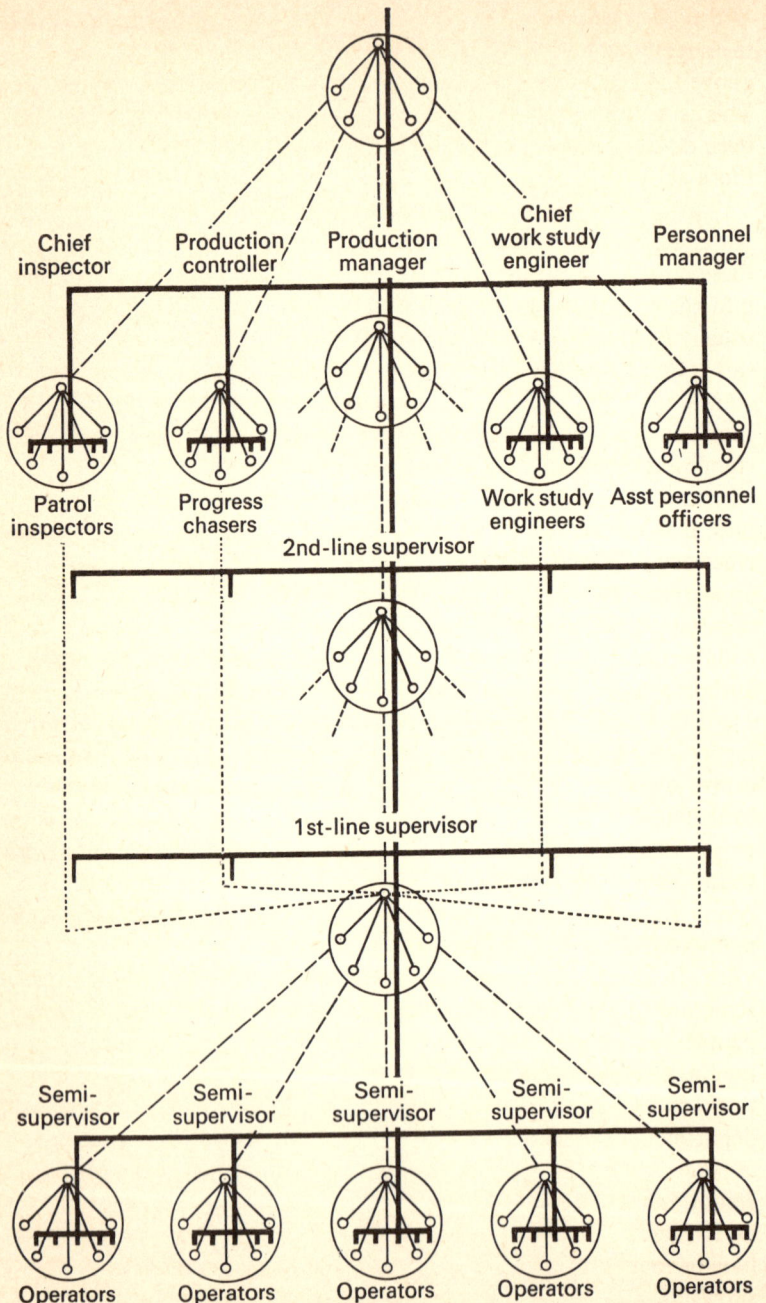

Chief inspector

Production controller

Production manager

Chief work study engineer

Personnel manager

Patrol inspectors

Progress chasers

2nd-line supervisor

Work study engineers

Asst personnel officers

1st-line supervisor

Semi-supervisor

Semi-supervisor

Semi-supervisor

Semi-supervisor

Semi-supervisor

Operators

Operators

Operators

Operators

Operators

FIG. 6. *Chart showing further functional links with the line*

of a typical company. And an important point to note here is that the supervisory manager has acquired a new relationship, over and above those with the person above him and his subordinates below. This is a kind of cross-link with the patrol inspector. And, as has been described above, it will be a different kind of relationship from those above and below.

In modern organization, these cross-links will tend to increase. All companies have problems at one time and another. And when these crop up, the obvious thing to do is to detail someone to look into them. If this person comes up with a workable plan, he will usually be given some help to put his plan into practice. Incidentally, this is quite often his first step in promotion, so when such a chance comes anyone's way, he should make the most of it. Thus, when someone is given the task of finding out why machines are not kept running to capacity, a production control department is well on the way to being established. When methods of work have to be looked into, a work study department is likely to be set up. When labour efficiency is questioned, a personnel department may soon make its appearance. But all these departments depend for their real effectiveness on the use the supervisor can make of them. Unless he can collaborate intelligently with them—and unless they support his authority and collaborate with him—they can remain a dead letter.

Fig. 6 shows an organization with a few more functional departments integrated into it. Inevitably the number of cross-links which centre on the supervisory manager will also increase. He now has functional relationships with a patrol inspector, a progress chaser, a work study engineer, and an assistant personnel officer. This may sound as though his job has become impossibly complicated. But running a present-day organization *is* a complicated business. And many of these complications inevitably centre on the first-line supervisor. In practice, however, it works out fairly well, so long as the structure of the organization is properly defined. So long as all the people concerned know where they stand in the organization; so long as they are clear about who is their immediate boss, and what they are responsible for; so long as they know what the functional departments are there for and how they operate; above all, so long as they are clear about the cross-links, things should go fairly smoothly. The ideal is to get as much as possible settled as low down as is practicable. This lets everyone get on with his job, without having to bother the people up above with a lot of detail. Fig. 7 shows a complete organization drawn out in detail, with the line and functional relationships outlined.

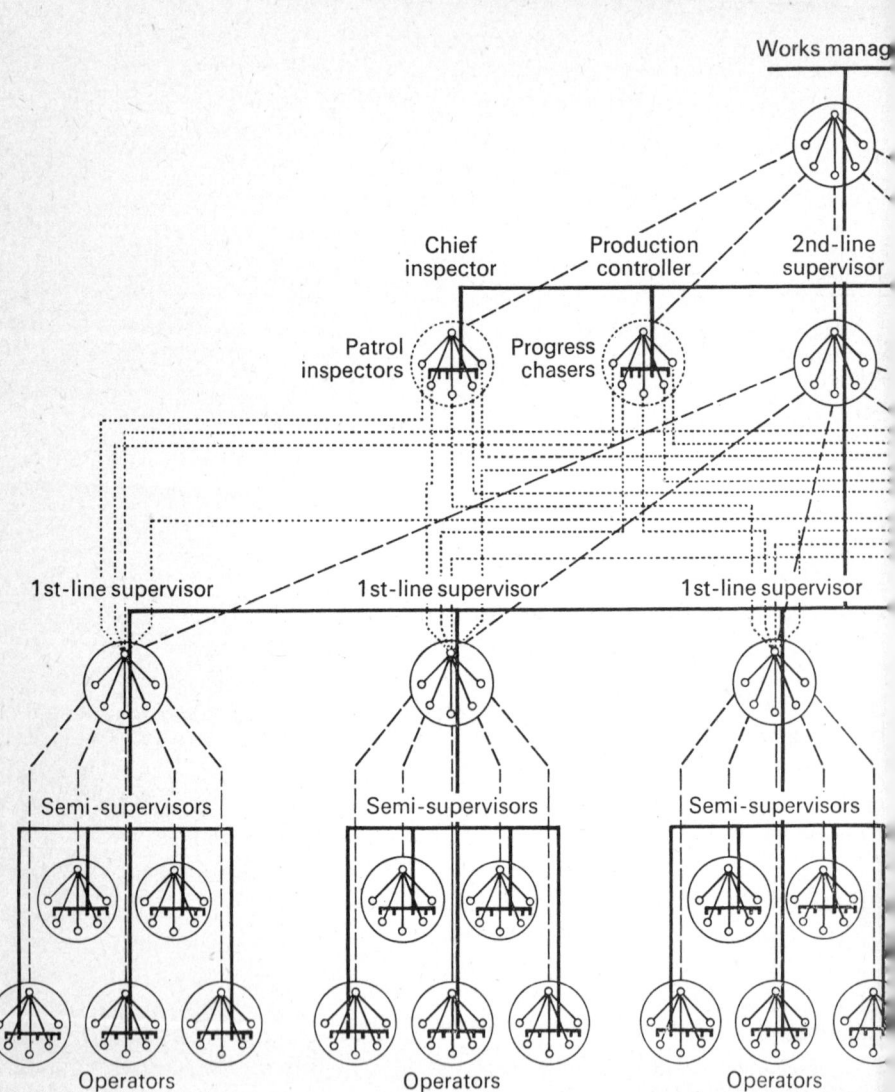

FIG. 7. *Chart showing organization with complete line and functional links*

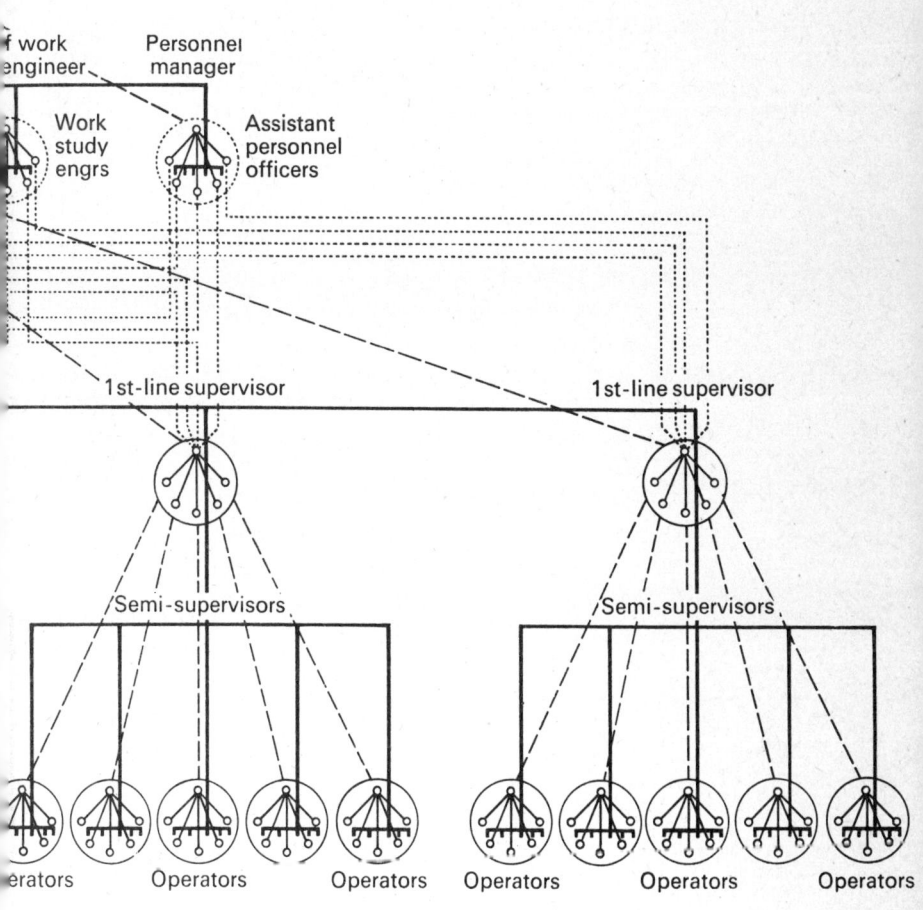

f work
engineer

Personnel
manager

Work
study
engrs

Assistant
personnel
officers

1st-line supervisor

1st-line supervisor

Semi-supervisors

Semi-supervisors

erators   Operators   Operators   Operators   Operators   Operators

Organization Theory

In recent years there has been a great deal of writing and thinking about organization. Theories have been put forward to explain how organizations come into being, and how they are adapted to different technologies. The kind of set-up that works in an oil refinery, for example, will not apply to a clothing factory. Different degrees of centralization are being studied, to show how far down the line decision making can be delegated. The effects of size on organization structure can also be important, for many problems seem to become more difficult to solve in the larger companies. Some of this theorizing may seem rather academic and far removed from the realities of day-to-day industrial work. A lot of it, however, is still in the early stages, and is more concerned with collecting information than with laying down the law.

Whatever form an organization takes, it will depend on human beings. And these human beings will have to work in relationships with each other. The structure will lay down the official patterns which these relationships ought to take. What concerns us, however, is how well these official patterns work in day-to-day practice. This will depend on how far the people concerned find these relationships rewarding and satisfying. If they do, they will put some effort into the roles required of them. If they don't, they will simply go through the motions until the bell rings. In situations like this, the amount of effort forthcoming is at its minimum.

Before we go into this, however, we should make quite clear what we mean when we talk about social roles and relationships. A *relationship* comes into being when two people enter into conversation, or talk to each other. For example:

A says to B: 'How do I get to the wages office?'
B replies: 'You go along to the end there. Up those stairs and turn to the left. Go down the passage and you'll find it at the second door on the left.'
A then says: 'Thanks very much. Second door on the left?'
B replies: 'That's right. You can't miss it.'

In this little interchange, A has become aware of B as a person. He has formed some impression of him, and also some expectations about how he will respond. In this case, he will probably think of him as a decent, helpful sort of chap. And if he has to speak to him again, he will expect him to behave in the same sort of way. The relationship which has come into being between A and B is thus of pretty good *quality*. Of course, if the conversation goes like this:

A: 'How do I get to the wages office?'

B: 'Why the hell ask me? D'you think I've nothing else to do but answer bloody silly questions all day?'

then the relationship will be of poor quality. A will think of B as a nasty-tempered so-and-so, and will avoid him whenever possible in future.

Social roles develop whenever relationships are continued for any length of time. Suppose, for example, B is the person in the organizational structure to whom A is supposed to go when he needs help or guidance. Then B has the role of 'helper out' towards A. Similarly A has the role of 'seeker for help' towards B. If every time A approaches B, he gets what he wants, then these roles will become natural and accepted. Similarly if A shows B a reasonable degree of appreciation for the help he gets, the roles will become still more satisfying to both parties. The relationship will grow into a good-quality, reliable one, because each can count on the other to carry out the role required of him.

The structure of any organization is built on the roles and relationships between the people who make it up. It will now be obvious what the effective working of that organization depends on. If the relationships within each pattern or sub-grouping are of good quality, people will be able to talk freely and confidently to each other. If the social roles are accepted and understood, people will be able to rely on each other to do what they expect of them. This may sound simple enough, and when we come down to first principles, it *is* simple and straightforward. However, there are complications.

Above the operator level, everyone has more than one social role. The supervisory manager, for example, has the role of task allocator, helper out, and adviser to his operators. He has the role of instruction receiver and information supplier to the manager above. He also has the role of intelligent collaborator with the functional specialists to whom he is cross-linked. Each of these has different expectations of him, while he in turn expects different things of them. He will thus have to drop one role and pick up another continuously throughout the day. And if he gets the roles mixed up—if he starts giving orders to his boss or allowing himself to be pushed around by his subordinates—things will go badly wrong.

But, you may say, this is what he's paid to do. That may be true enough, though whether the supervisory manager understood what he was letting himself in for when he accepted promotion may be another matter. But when we think of this aspect of organization, we must consider what people get out of the social roles we have offered them in the structure.

Rewards of social roles. In some cases, these are quite straight-forward. We can say to an operator: 'We want you to carry out this task over and over again for 8 hours a day. And if you keep up a set standard, we'll pay you so much at the end of the week.' The operator needs the money, so he accepts the job. Is there any reason why both sides should not be satisfied with the transaction?

After a few days in the job, some such reasons may make themselves felt. The operator needs the money all right. But once he is earning a regular wage, this need will fade into the background—as needs do as soon as they are satisfied. He will then become aware of other needs. The need for friendly relationships with other people, for example, during the 8 hours he spends at work. Does the role we have offered to him in the organization satisfy this need? A lot will depend on its structure at the lowest level. If he is a member of a small working team, his role may well satisfy him. This is what the social psychologist calls a *primary group*, where the relationships are flexible and informal. And where the individual has a role in a good-quality pattern centring on a semi-supervisor, such a role can satisfy another need as well. This is the need to count as an individual, to be appreciated by other people, and to feel that they recognize the importance of what one is doing. By satisfying this need, these primary groups can draw out a lot more effort from people at work.

But if the role offered is unrewarding in these senses—if the operator is a member of a *secondary group* with a set task in a large pattern of impersonal relationships—then a different set of results can be expected. He will think: 'All I'm getting out of this is money. I don't count for anything as a person in this set-up. I'm just a cog in the machine.' This is where the unofficial pattern of relationships will form—the small clique which gossips together in the tea break, or the informal 'me and my mates' group, where the individual feels he is accepted as a member. Such groups offer informal roles which satisfy the need to belong and to be appreciated that the role in the formal structure does not. And they can easily become the focus of anti-organization activities—limitation of output, unwarranted demarcation of jobs, working to rule, and all the rest of it.

We should think, then, of the kinds of satisfaction an operator can get from the working role we offer him. And if we decide that it offers money and nothing else, we should perhaps reconsider the factory floor structure of our organization. Above this level, of course, the working role of the supervisory manager offers a lot more.

He is a central figure, to whom other people refer for advice, guidance, or information. He cannot help feeling a significant figure, and one on whom the structure depends. Whether he feels he is getting enough money may be another question. No one can ever be fully satisfied anyway, for human beings can always envisage a higher level. This is what progress depends on, and we should always try to provide opportunities for these higher levels of aspiration.

There is just one final point. Roles and relationships are interdependent between individuals. Thus, if A takes an authoritarian, bullying role towards B, he is offering him only two choices. B can either submit and feel bitter and hostile towards A, or he can stand up to him and have a good old up-and-downer. Neither of these two roles gives B much chance of making a constructive contribution towards the purpose of the organization. Both arouse emotional reactions, which act like grit in its works. It would be better, therefore, if A approached B in such a way as to offer him a self-respecting role as a responsible colleague. B could then meet him half-way, and get some satisfaction out of the interchange. If the members of an organization are aware of these processes, its structure will work effectively. In fact, even a not-very-good structure will operate, if its members can handle their roles and relationships within it. But if these roles and relationships go wrong, even the perfect structure will fall apart in a very short time.

SUMMARY

1 *What is the meaning of the term 'line organization'?*

The line organization shows the various levels of authority as they go down from the chief executive to the operator on the job. It also outlines the areas of responsibility at each level. The conventional way of illustrating the line organization is by the T-chart.

2 *What are the limitations of T-charts?*

They do not show up the groupings into which the relationships between the people at each level must fall. Nor do they emphasize the importance of free and effective communication within and between these groupings. This is most important at the lower levels in a large organization. Charting organizations at these lower levels, however, is difficult because of the amount of detail which has to be included. Organizational structure thus tends to become rather indefinite where it is most important that it should be most clearly defined.

3 *What levels of responsibility are found in any organization?*

 (a) *The operator*, who is responsible for his own task and nothing more.
 (b) *The semi-supervisor*, who is still doing an operator's job but has a little responsibility for a few others around him.
 (c) *The first-line supervisor*, not doing an operator's job, but responsible full-time for the work of others.
 (d) *Second- and third-line supervisors*, in charge of those on the first line, but still interpreting rules and policies.
 (e) *Middle management*, concerned with the initiation of new developments, with more liberty of action.
 (f) *Higher management*, concerned with long-range planning and less with day-to-day running.

4 *What is a functional or specialist department?*

A functional or specialist department has been set up to study one particular aspect of an organization's activities. Its responsibility for this activity may run throughout the whole of the organization. The most typical functional departments are inspection (or quality control), production control, work study, maintenance, cost control, and personnel.

5 *How do functional or specialist departments fit into the line organization?*

At the top level they will be responsible to the chief executive, while within each there will be a line organization with subordinates responsible at each level to the person above. The main problem, however, is the fitting of the lower functional specialists into the groups responsible to the line supervisors. This will depend on an understanding on their part that the line supervisor has overall charge within his area of responsibility. It will also depend on the supervisor's understanding of the specialist's function, and his ability to collaborate intelligently with him.

6 *What do we mean by the roles and relationships within an organization?*

A *relationship* comes into being when two people interact together. Each becomes aware of the other as a person and develops expectations of how he will behave. A social *role* develops when relationships become established, and consist of the behaviour expected of the people involved in these relationships. Relationships can vary in quality. The structure of an organization consists of the formal roles and relationships expected of the people who make it up.

7 *What do people get out of their roles at work?*

People are paid for the social roles they occupy during working hours. If, however, they get nothing more than money for carrying out a set and rather boring task for eight hours in the day, they will not be satisfied. They expect some feelings of friendliness from their relationships at work, and also some kind of appreciation for what they do. If these additional satisfactions are not provided by the roles they occupy in the formal structure of organization, informal relationships and groupings are likely to come into existence which provide these rewards. Such informal groupings can frequently cut across the formal organizational structure.

8 *What sort of role is offered to the supervisory manager?*

He occupies a central role on which other people's roles depend. How they play their roles towards him will be determined by how he behaves towards them, for roles are interdependent. The supervisory role cannot fail to offer the satisfaction of a sense of belonging to the organization and occupying an important place within it.

CHAPTER 4 | Supervisory Duties and Responsibilities

No two supervisory management jobs will ever be exactly the same. There are different types of product and different methods of production. There are jobs which do not involve production at all; maintenance or erection supervisors, office or administrative supervisors. Each firm has its own way of working and its own organizational set-up. Each firm has its own atmosphere and each is dependent on the personalities of its senior staff. Can one say anything worth-while that will apply to all supervisory management jobs?

Whatever the job supervised, there will be certain common elements in the responsibility of the supervisory manager. These can be classified under three headings:

Technical, or concerned with the actual processes and tasks to be supervised.
Operational, or concerned with the control and recording of these processes.
Personnel, or concerned with the human beings who carry out the processes.

These can never be kept completely separate from each other. Nevertheless, they provide a useful framework, and we shall deal with them in turn.

Technical Aspects
These, of course, will vary with the type of production. Joan Woodward, however, has provided us with a useful classification for these. She suggests three basic types:

(a) One-off or small-batch production
(b) Large-batch or flow production
(c) Process production or automation

These are not perhaps all-inclusive, but the reader should find that his type of work fits fairly easily into one or the other.

One-off or small-batch production. This very largely explains itself. It involves the making of products to special orders, either one at a time or in small lots. This kind of production usually calls for a good deal of skill on the part of the operator. He is not working to a fixed routine, but is meeting the special problems presented by each job. From the supervisory point of view, it calls for an even greater degree of technical knowledge. For whenever the operator comes up against a difficulty he cannot solve, he must be able to fall back on the man in charge of him. And he must have confidence that he will get the answer from him.

In one-off production, it is practically certain that the supervisory manager must have been promoted from the job itself, and that he himself must be skilled in the jobs he is supervising. One must emphasize, of course, that this is only one part of his qualifications, and that the foreman who claims: 'I can do any job in this shop better than any of the men under me' is not necessarily the best foreman. In fact, this concentration on only one aspect of his task may be a limitation. Without this skill and practical experience, however, he will be under a handicap.

In the first place, he will not be able to think of alternative ways of doing the job when the operator gets stuck. In practice, this means that when the operator comes to him and says: 'I've been working on this so-and-so all morning and I'm just not getting anywhere,' the supervisory manager should be able to say: 'Yes, I thought you might have difficulty with that one. Have you tried it this way?' If the operator then says: 'Blimey, I never thought of that. I think that'd do it,' then the supervisory manager has fulfilled his function. He has gone that one stage further, after the operator has run out of ideas.

In the second place, he must know what is practicable and what isn't. This applies not only to getting the job done, but also to the risks and dangers involved. Safety is one of the supervisory manager's responsibilities. And if someone comes along with a bright idea, he must not only know whether or not it will work in practice. He must also know what risks it involves to life and property. If he considers these unjustified, he must turn the idea down. And he cannot know this without a background of practical experience.

Thirdly, he must have the confidence of the operators under him. And he will never retain this if they feel they know more than he does. Part of this knowledge will be practical and based on experience as outlined above. Part will be technical or theoretical. If the reading of drawings is involved, he must have some grasp of the principles of draughtsmanship. When in charge of machine tools or other complex equipment, he must understand their design and capacities. If strict tolerances are called for, he must know the relevant methods of measurement, and the standard of accuracy that these permit. Over and above all this, he must have some idea of the next step ahead, so that when a new machine or a new process appears, he isn't caught scratching his head and saying: 'Well, whatever will they think of next?' In other words, he must know just that little bit more than the operators under him about everything that affects the technical aspect of the job. This will quickly become obvious to them and they will respect him for it.

Large-batch or flow production. As soon as any product catches on and can be sold in quantity, management will be keen to change the method of production. Making things one at a time is always expensive. It involves skilled labour; the rate of overhead recovery is low; the items take up space; and they take a long time to pass through the shop. If only the process could be speeded up, it would be much more satisfactory.

The answer to this is flow production, which depends on the following steps.

Standardization of the product. This means that each one can be handled in exactly the same way. As everyone knows, Henry Ford was one of the apostles of flow production. His Model T was a standard car, each example of which went through an exactly similar production process. His famous crack: 'They can have any colour they like, so long as it's black' illustrates this. Nowadays, of course, variations can be introduced into a flow line—different colours, different types of upholstery, automatic gearboxes, and so on. These, however, are still designed so that they all can be fitted in a similar manner. The essential characteristic of standardization remains, even though a range of variations can now be produced.

Standard method of production. Once the product has been standardized, the method of making it can be broken down into a series of steps. These again can be standardized, so that at each stage an exactly similar process is carried out. Successive steps can be balanced against each other so that one fits exactly with the next. Where quantities and expense justify it, this can result in a moving assembly line, on which a series of operations are carried out on a flow of standard products as they pass along.

Standardized semi-skilled jobs. By now, the need for a skilled man has disappeared. Each stage in the production process has been turned into a simplified task, carried out over and over again according to routine, on the standardized product. These tasks can be learnt in a comparatively short time. They allow no room for judgment or initiative on the part of the operator. The main demand they make is that the operator keeps up with the line, and does not slow it down or stop the flow of production.

Final assembly lines in a motor car plant are the most dramatic examples of flow production. However, the same principles can be applied in any type of industry. As soon as the batches to be produced rise above a certain size, some move in the direction of flow production can be made. The job can be broken down into stages, and each stage can be turned into a standardized task.

It will be obvious that in flow production the supervisory manager is faced with a different kind of technical problem. Experience on any one of the jobs he supervises is of little use to him, because none of these calls for skill or judgment. In fact, the whole point about flow production is that the skill and judgment has been engineered out of the individual jobs. The technical demands on the supervisory manager are more like those on a production engineer. He must be able to see the process as a whole, and to appreciate the need for keeping it going. He must, in fact, become flow-minded.

The technical expertise in flow production centres on the process, rather than on the individual jobs. Thus the supervisory manager should find it comparatively easy to move from one type of product to another. He might, in fact, move from one industry to another, for the principles do not change. Motor cars, washing machines, men's suits, household furniture, food products—these and a host of other articles are pouring off the production lines to make our society more and more affluent.

The technical demands of the one-off job may have disappeared from the flow production line, but the supervisory manager's technical responsibility still remains. Now, however, it is less a matter of being able to put things right himself. His job is rather to recognize when something is going wrong, and to know the right person to call on to deal with it. The days when the enthusiastic amateur was encouraged to tinker about with complex machinery are long past. We now recognize such people as a menace, who do more damage than they put right. Nowadays, we call on trained and experienced maintenance mechanics who can locate the fault, replace the defective component, and get the equipment back into service with the minimum delay. Over and above this, there is, of course, the need for regular servicing and overhaul when the line is out of production.

Process or automated production. As flow production develops, jobs become more simple and repetitive until they require little or no skill or experience. Finally there comes a point where jobs disappear altogether. Someone invents a mechanism which can carry out the task, and can be fitted into the process. This is where the transition from flow production to automation takes place. The semi-skilled jobs have been replaced by automatic-transfer machinery. And instead of a line of operators doing standardized, repetitive jobs, we have a bank of complex equipment centring on a control panel. One man watches the dials which record what is going on, and presses the switches to start and stop the various operations.

The wheel has now turned full circle. The skilled craftsman on the one-off job gave way to the semi-skilled operator on the flow production line. He in turn gave way to the technician controlling the automated process. Once again, it is dangerous to generalize, but the process operator is likely to be a different kind of person again. He will need a high level of qualifications if he is to control the equipment he is in charge of effectively. These qualifications will be different from the skills of the craftsman, and are likely to include some theoretical understanding of the process and the plant. Any ideas that the process worker merely watches a dial and presses a button are dangerously misleading. If he presses the wrong button, or presses the right button at the wrong time, the results could be disastrous.

The technical responsibilities of the supervisory manager will also change in nature. Once again, he must be able to take over when the operator's knowledge comes to an end. Thus, his understanding of the process and the equipment will probably have to reach the standard of a recognized technical qualification.

As we move from one-off through flow production to automation, the relative proportions of labour and equipment in the final product have changed. In one-off production, the job may depend on highly skilled craftsmen working with hand tools. This is known as a *labour-intensive* situation. Most of the value in the final product comes from the skill of the craftsman. A large part of the cost will accordingly be the wages of these craftsmen. Consequently, if the supervisory manager's technical expertise can economize on the use of this skilled labour, or if he can utilize it more efficiently, he will play a large part in cutting the cost of the product.

As flow production or automation takes the place of the one-off job, however, the proportion of capital equipment will increase. Thus the job becomes more *capital-intensive*, with a larger part of the cost accounted for by the plant and machinery. In this situation, the supervisory manager's main contribution to economy is to keep the plant running. A hold-up of even a few minutes in a plant costing several hundred thousand pounds can be an expensive business. This is even more obvious when a number of sub-processes are integrated into one organization. In these cases a stoppage in one small department can bring the whole show to a standstill.

The technical responsibilities of the supervisory manager can thus be extremely varied. As has been said, they will depend, in the first place, on the industry and the type of product. In a book like this, there is nothing we can usefully say about these. But quite apart from the actual industry, there will be differences according to the method of production. In the one-off shops, practical experience and know-how will enable the supervisor to deal effectively with the technical aspects of his job. And for these, there will be no substitute. But one-off jobs tend to give way to flow production—at least in firms which are going ahead in their marketing and production methods. These changes will modify the supervisory manager's technical responsibility. And his practical experience and know-how may no longer serve the same purpose. He may find himself relying more and more on maintenance mechanics and production engineers. He may have to learn and appreciate their ways of thinking. This does not mean that his technical responsibilities have disappeared, or indeed grown any less. They have simply changed in nature. And most supervisory managers will be faced with several of these changes in the course of their working life. They had better start preparing for them and trying to anticipate them in their own industries.

Operational Responsibilities

Industry, as we have said, is the organization of men, machinery, and materials, all of which cost money. These can be arranged in different orders of importance according to the situation. They can be organized on a large scale, which is the task of higher management. But they must also be organized on a small, day-to-day scale, which is the task of supervisory management. This may be less glamorous and exciting than when the Board of ICI is planning a multi-million-pound development, but it can be no less important in the successful running of a firm.

How this day-to-day planning looks in practice may be illustrated by the following imaginary conversation. The middle manager drops in on one of his subordinates and asks: 'How's that job for Smith and Brown going?'

The supervisory manager replies: 'I've had to stop it. The milling cutter needs setting for the new tolerances.'

'Well, can't you get a mechanic on it? It's pretty urgent.'

'I know. But the mechanic's busy on the jig-borer. We need that

for the export order. And I've got to get that cleared to make room
for the new job you told me about yesterday.'

'Oh yes. That's right. But what's Charlie doing in the mean-
time? He's not just standing around waiting for the mechanic, I
hope?'

'Oh, no. I've put him on the Jones and Robinson order.'

'What on earth did you do that for? It's not all that urgent.
That South American order's much more important. We could get
a lot of new business out of that one.'

'I know. But we're waiting for those components for that one.
You remember, I told you about them last week.'

'So you did. My God! Can't we ever do anything right in this
place?'

This would be a typically quiet morning in the life of a supervisory manager. With any luck, he might satisfy his boss that he had
worked out the best way of running things at the moment: that he
was making the best use of his *machine* capacity; that he was keeping
his *men* fully occupied; that he was adequately utilizing the *materials*
available; and that he was not wasting the *money* which all these are
costing.

This is what we describe as the operational side of the supervisory manager's job. In some of the textbooks, it is called the
administrative side, but this is not a particularly attractive word.
'Administration' calls to mind a picture of important people sitting
in offices and thinking up ways of making other peoples' jobs more
difficult. 'Operational' is a better word, for it gives more of an
impression of getting things done. And this is what the supervisory
manager is really there for. Whatever word we use, however, the task
is still one of the most important in the organization. Men and
machines have got to be kept at work. Material has got to be kept
flowing through into finished products. And once again the supervisory manager is the key man. He is on the spot in more senses than
one. He takes the blame if things go wrong. And he should get the
credit if they go right.

This is an area of management where definite objectives can be
set. And the effectiveness of individuals can be measured in terms of
these objectives. There are advantages in this, because, from one
point of view, the individual is getting a fairer deal. He is being
judged, not by whether his face fits or his boss thinks he's a nice chap,
but on his actual performance on the job—this performance being
measured against an objective standard. The disadvantages, of
course, are that it becomes more difficult to get away with anything.

Little off-the-record wangles tend to come to light, to the embarrass-
ment of all concerned. Sooner or later, however, most firms have to
face up to some measurement of their operational efficiency. And if
a supervisory manager has got used to the idea beforehand, he'll find
it less of a shock.

Using Plant

The aim of any organization should be to have all its plant
operating during every hour of the working day at maximum
capacity. This is a matter where measurement is comparatively easy.
Suppose, for example, we have a department with twenty-five
machines, each capable of an output of fifty units an hour. This
gives us a total capacity of 1,250 units an hour. Suppose, also, that
this department is working an 8-hour day. It would therefore be
theoretically capable of producing 10,000 units a day.

But, you may say, that is just theoretical nonsense. To get such
an output, each machine would have to be running at full speed from
the moment we start work. And it would have to carry on at this
speed right up until the bell rings. That's just not possible. There's
got to be a certain amount of down-time, for setting, changing
models, and so on. Chaps have got to go off the job now and then,
for reasons we don't need to go into here. You'd never get 10,000
units a day out of that department, not in a million years. So, what's
the point of working out a figure like that in the first place, if it can
never be reached in practice?

Well, let's look at it this way. On each day of the week the actual
output of the department was as follows:

Monday	7,500 units, or 75% of the theoretically possible
Tuesday	8,000 „ 80% „ „ „
Wednesday	9,500 „ 95% „ „ „
Thursday	8,500 „ 85% „ „ „
Friday	8,000 „ 80% „ „ „

This gives us a standard, or a benchmark, against which to
measure the actual output. And, instead of saying: 'Things seem to
have gone pretty well on Wednesday, whereas on Monday output
fell off a bit,' we can now say: 'On Wednesday, output was within
5% of what is theoretically possible, while on no other day was it
within 15% of that figure. On Monday it was 25% off and on Tuesday
and Friday it was 20% off.' With this objective measurement to go
on, we are in a much better position to evaluate performance. And,
of course, we shall immediately be led to think of the reasons for

these variations. We may, in fact, rumble that Wednesday is the day on which the week's piecework earnings are added up—and that this is the reason why the chaps are working extra hard to make sure their money's all right for the end of the week.

Management by Objectives
Management by objectives like this is really an attitude of mind —one which welcomes any form of measurement and thinks of the uses that can be made of it. And it is the attitude which the modern supervisory manager must try to acquire. This is not always easy for him. Very often his close contact with day-to-day problems causes him to be more aware of the difficulties. In one rather light-hearted guide to consultancy, there was a series of definitions. This included:

'The *foreman*—the man who says it can't be done.'

Such cracks shouldn't be taken too seriously, but they have a certain significance. They illustrate the difference between the outlook of someone who can't see beyond the problems of day-to-day working, and the chap who can sit back and try to sum up the situation as a whole.

The supervisory manager's operational task should be to get as near the theoretically possible output from his machines as he can. If regular records are kept, a figure for this will usually make its appearance. In the example quoted, 95% was the highest reached. And it may be that over a period this figure is never exceeded. As a working rule, therefore, it could perhaps be taken that this is the best practical performance that can be expected.

How to reach this best practical performance will involve planning. And this again will depend on the type of production of which the supervisory manager is in charge. In a one-off shop, he will be presented with a continuous series of problems. Different jobs will be coming through, each with its own demands on machine time. Machines may require setting up for each job. The task of keeping them all operating, while at the same time getting the jobs through on time, will be a difficult one. But it is one of the supervisory manager's major responsibilities. He must find time to sit back and think about it. Some form of diagram may be helpful, for this will make it easier to see the problem as a whole, rather than as a series of on-the-spot crises.

In a large-batch or flow production shop, this problem of machine utilization may be rather easier. Or, at least, the supervisory manager may be able to rely on more help from outside his department. Here the difference between one-off and flow production makes itself felt. High standards of machine utilization are seldom possible in a one-off shop. The whole set-up is against it, and the planning and costing will have taken this factor into account. The main idea behind flow production, on the other hand, is high machine utilization. The organization should therefore have been planned with this in mind. A production control department will be included in the set-up. And one of its main responsibilities will be to plan programmes for each production department to keep the plant fully occupied.

But it is one thing to plan a programme, and quite another to ensure that it has been put into practice. Who is the key man here? Once again, it's the supervisory manager. He gets his programme at the beginning of the week. This provides for some nice long runs that will keep his plant busy, without stopping for alterations in the settings or changes in models. On Monday, everything looks all set for a peaceful week's working.

The production control department, however, has not only got to think about machine utilization. It's concerned with deliveries to customers as well. Sometimes the two responsibilities can cut across each other, and one or other has to go by the board. When the market is in favour of the seller and customers are queueing up, deliveries can take second place to machine utilization. But when the firm is scratching round for orders, or when an important customer wants something urgently, deliveries become more important. Then someone from production control comes down into the department and says: 'You'll have to fit this job in. It's very urgent.' Once again we're back to the same problem of the relation of the functional specialist to the line organization.

The supervisory manager may respond: 'My God. Can't you so-and-sos ever stick to anything for more than 5 minutes? Here am I, all set up for the programme you put out yesterday. And no sooner do we get started than you come down wanting to change it all round.' All quite justifiable from his point of view, and perhaps taken as no more than a harmless blowing off of steam by the progress chaser. But once again we have the beginnings of trouble, if the two people concerned cannot work out an amicable solution. This is real life at the level of the supervisory manager. And these are the real problems which he must face in his job.

Using Materials
Production machinery does not run by itself. It needs raw

material to work on. To get maximum machine utilization, you need a continuous flow of raw material.

Raw material varies from one process to another. Iron ore, extracted from the earth, is a raw material for the iron and steel industry. Raw wool, clipped from the backs of sheep, plays the same part in the wool textile industry. Wheat grain is the raw material of the flour-milling industry. These are raw materials in the 'rawest' sense of the word. They are natural products—or primary products —and they go in at the start of the manufacturing process.

These raw materials go through a manufacturing operation in one organization and become a finished product. But these finished products become the raw material of the next process. To transform iron ore into sheet steel involves a number of steps and a great deal of very expensive plant. But sheet steel itself is simply the raw material for car bodies, metal boxes, and a number of other manufactured goods. Similarly, when raw wool is spun into yarn, it becomes the raw material for the clothing trades. Wheat grain, milled into flour, is the raw material for the baking industry, and so on.

The supply of raw material can be thought of as a series of stages in a vast industrial process. At one end are the mines, the cornfields, and the grazing cattle. At the other are the motor cars, the fashionable clothes, and the well-cooked appetizing meals. In between are a series of extractive, manufacturing, and distributive stages. And our standard of living is simply the speed at which the whole process flows. The ideal is to push it as fast as it can go. Anything that stands still is slowing the process down. And any slowing down means less goods to buy and less money to buy them with.

All this may seem a little far away from the supervisory manager's job in the individual factory. But it is as well to bear this background in mind. It helps to fit things into place and put them in perspective. What the individual firm is trying to do is to keep its place in this flow of production and distribution. And the supervisory manager is keeping the flow going in his own particular department. He should think about what is coming in at one end; what processes it is going through; and what goes out at the other end. And he should be thinking all the time about how he can speed up the flow.

An adequate supply of raw material is one of the essential elements in this flow, and it would be nice to think that the firm had an enormous store filled with a year's supply of everything it could possibly need. There are, however, two snags to this. One is the cost: for raw material, like everything else in industry, costs money. And to tie up thousands, or even hundreds of thousands, of pounds in raw material is not the way to run a business. Money usually has to be borrowed, and the rate of interest nowadays is fairly high. Thus, if a firm has £100,000 tied up in stocks and the rate of interest is 7%, this represents a yearly charge of £7,000. And even half of that would make a nice addition to a supervisory manager's salary.

The other point is that all this stuff is standing still. As we pointed out above, anything standing still is slowing down the whole economic process. We must always keep in mind the ideal of a continuous flow—of materials flowing smoothly through each manufacturing unit; of the partially finished products of one flowing into the next; of their passing smoothly through its productive processes; of the finished goods flowing into the hands of customers; and of their money flowing back through the whole system; remembering always that it is the money that makes it all work.

Stocks, therefore, should always be kept as low as possible in order to cut down the money tied up in them. On the other hand, we must never risk running short, for this would bring production to a standstill. Measurements come in useful here again, and the various factors in the situation can be brought under control. Take the following example.

In a particular department, the week's requirements of raw material will be 1,000 units. The time required for delivery, between placing the order and receiving the supplies, will be 2 weeks. Thus whenever the stock gets down to 2 weeks' supply (2,000 units) an order must be placed for a further delivery. This, however, leaves no margin for error, and if there is a slip-up anywhere along the line we shall be in trouble. Orders may be delayed; deliveries may be held up; there may be transport difficulties. We had better allow for these by always having a week's supply in hand. This will give us our *re-order level*, which in this case will be:

Delivery time (2 weeks) × weekly requirements (1,000)+1 week's margin of error (1,000) = 3,000 units

There will be a standing instruction, therefore, that whenever the stock drops to 3,000, an order for a further supply must be placed.

What size should this order be? This will depend on several factors, one of which will be the most convenient amount for delivery. Suppose that, in this example, 5,000 units makes a convenient lorry load. Other things being equal, this would be the right quantity to order at a time. From the stores point of view they would seldom need space for more than 6,000 units of this type of material (6 weeks' supply), while their minimum stock would be round about

1,000, or 1 week's supply. It might be possible to arrange for some kind of danger signal when the stock fell below that level, for then the risk of running short and stopping production is beginning to make itself felt.

This example should make clear the principles of stock control. These, of course, will have to be applied to particular situations. In some, the delivery period may be longer and the quantities correspondingly larger. In others, they may be shorter, the minimum stocks lower, and the whole flow speeded up. In others again, it may be difficult to rely on delivery dates being adhered to, and the margin of error will have to be increased. Each case will present its own problems, but the underlying aim will remain the same.

Within the department, the same principles will apply, though here we think of raw material rather as *work-in-progress*. And this gives the quickest clue to the efficiency of a factory. If, when you walk through, you see large piles of work-in-progress lying about, you should sell your shares at once. This is costing money, just as too much material in store is costing money. In the efficiently run factory, everything is on the move, passing as rapidly as possible through the production process into finished goods. Just as the supervisory manager should make sure that all his machines are fully occupied, so he should keep material and work-in-progress on the move as well.

SUMMARY

1 *How can we classify the duties and responsibilities of the supervisory manager?*

Whatever the firm or the industry, the following elements will be found in any supervisory job:

Technical, or concerned with the processes and tasks to be supervised.
Operational, or concerned with the control and recording of these processes.
Personnel, or concerned with the human beings who carry out the tasks and processes.

2 *What are the supervisory manager's technical responsibilities in one-off or small-batch production?*

In these cases the tasks will be carried out by skilled craftsmen working on one job at a time. The supervisor will have to make on-the-spot decisions about methods of work, and about what is practicable and can safely be undertaken. Operators must be able to rely on him for technical help and guidance on the job, and to retain their confidence he must have considerable experience and knowledge of the tasks themselves. He must also have a grasp of the theoretical and technical issues involved. In addition, he should be ready to meet new developments in machines, processes, or material.

3 *What are the supervisory manager's technical responsibilities in large-batch or flow production?*

This type of production depends on standardization of products and production methods, and calls for semi-skilled operators working on standard tasks. Experience on such tasks will be of less value to the supervisor. His job is to keep production flowing, and this demands more knowledge of the process as a whole, and the ability to call on the appropriate specialist when anything threatens to interrupt the flow.

4 *What are the supervisory manager's technical responsibilities in process or automated production?*

When flow production becomes completely standardized, the semi-skilled jobs are replaced by automated processes. The operator then becomes a technician controlling the process, usually by electronic apparatus. Production has now become capital-intensive rather than labour-intensive. The supervisor needs a high standard of technological knowledge and insight to be able to control the process as a whole.

5 *What are the supervisory manager's operational responsibilities?*

He must make full use of the *machine* capacity entrusted to him.
He must utilize the available *materials* economically.
He must keep his *men* fully occupied.
He must keep an eye on the *money* which all these are costing.

6 *What does management by objectives mean?*

The output of which a plant is theoretically capable can be calculated, and allowance made for setting up or other down-time. Production control can plan a programme to keep this plant fully occupied and at the same time meet delivery requirements. On this basis a measurable objective can be set for the supervisory manager in charge, and his success judged by how far he meets these figures.

7 *How does materials utilization concern the supervisory manager?*

Materials cost money, and money lying idle is an unnecessary expense in any business. The aim, therefore, should be to work on minimum stocks, while at the same time avoiding any risk of running short. This can be calculated by relating weekly utilization to delivery dates and setting a re-order level which allows for economic quantities and a margin of error. In the same way work-in-progress should be kept on the move, so that the money it represents is passing as quickly as possible through the production process.

The technical and operational aspects of supervision are important. But more often than not the key to success lies in the handling of the personnel aspect. Here the supervisory manager is very much on his own. Functional or specialist departments can give help on technical or production problems. But the best personnel department in the world will never be able to support the supervisor who cannot manage the people under his charge. It is in this area that his personal qualities and judgment will play the greatest part. He must do everything he can to develop these qualities and deepen his insight into what makes people tick. We shall be touching on different aspects of this in the following chapters, as we consider the supervisory manager's personnel responsibilities from different points of view. First, however, we must get this function into focus.

The personnel function of management covers all aspects which involve people. You may object that there is no aspect of management which does not involve people in one way or another. And you could be quite right. But the process of planning, recruiting, and selecting staff; training them; and dealing with all the problems they present during working hours, can be looked at as a series of steps. These have been laid out in systematic form in Fig. 8. It may simplify things if we take these one at a time.

Manpower Planning

The first step is to decide what we want. Starting from scratch with a well-planned organization, this should be straightforward. We should know that we need so many higher and middle managers, of different grades and different specialist experience. We shall want so many supervisory managers capable of taking charge of the various sections. We shall want so many operators with the skills required by the factory floor jobs. Working this out from the organization chart will present few problems. It will simply be a matter of adding up the numbers in each category.

Organizations should not remain static, however. If they do, they are in danger of being overtaken by others which develop and make progress. New methods of production, new techniques and equipment, new products for new markets will make their appearance. And unless we have the people who can handle these as they appear, we shall be caught with our pants down. Planning for the

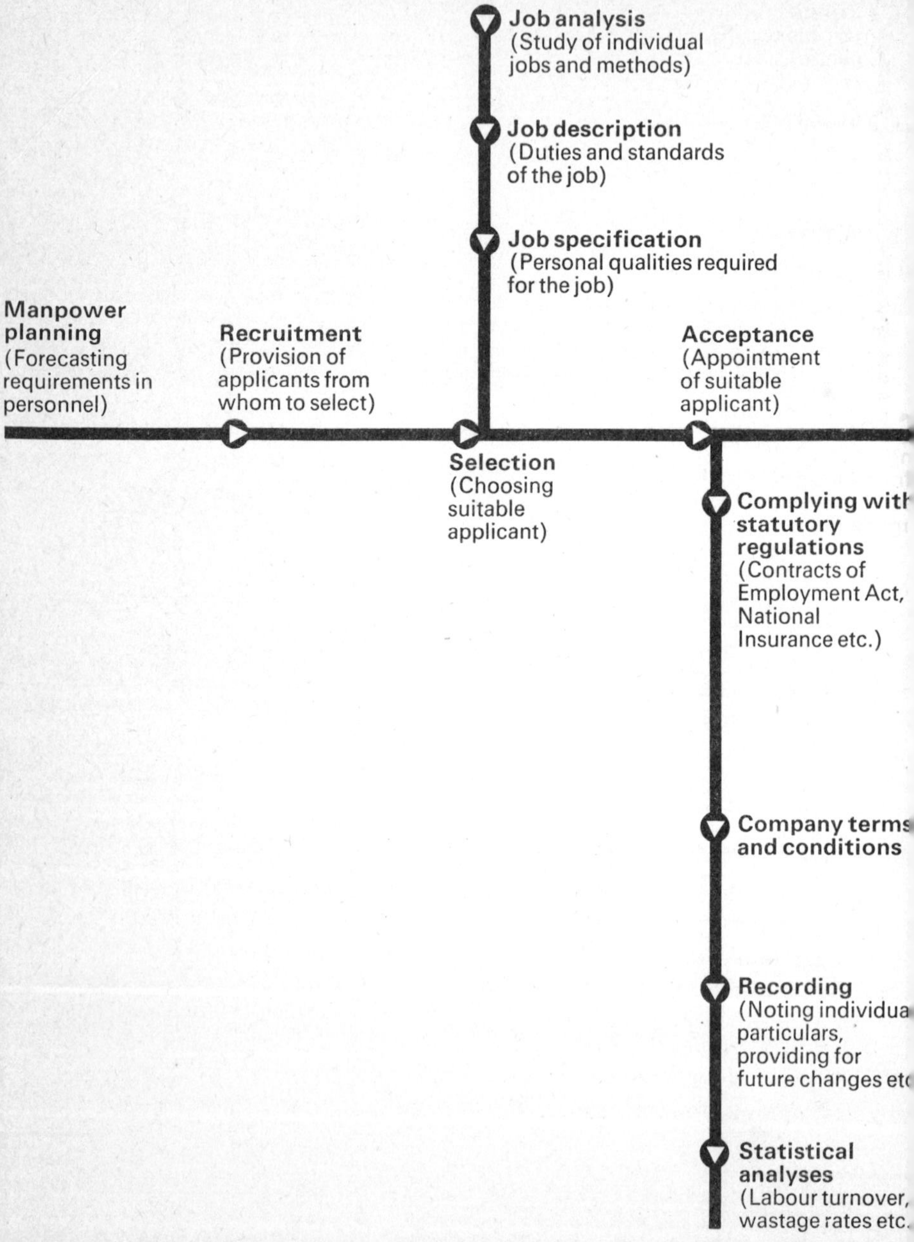

Job analysis
(Study of individual jobs and methods)

Job description
(Duties and standards of the job)

Job specification
(Personal qualities required for the job)

Manpower planning
(Forecasting requirements in personnel)

Recruitment
(Provision of applicants from whom to select)

Acceptance
(Appointment of suitable applicant)

Selection
(Choosing suitable applicant)

Complying with statutory regulations
(Contracts of Employment Act, National Insurance etc.)

Company terms and conditions

Recording
(Noting individual particulars, providing for future changes etc.)

Statistical analyses
(Labour turnover, wastage rates etc.)

FIG. 8. *Systematic approach to the personnel function (excluding industrial relations)*

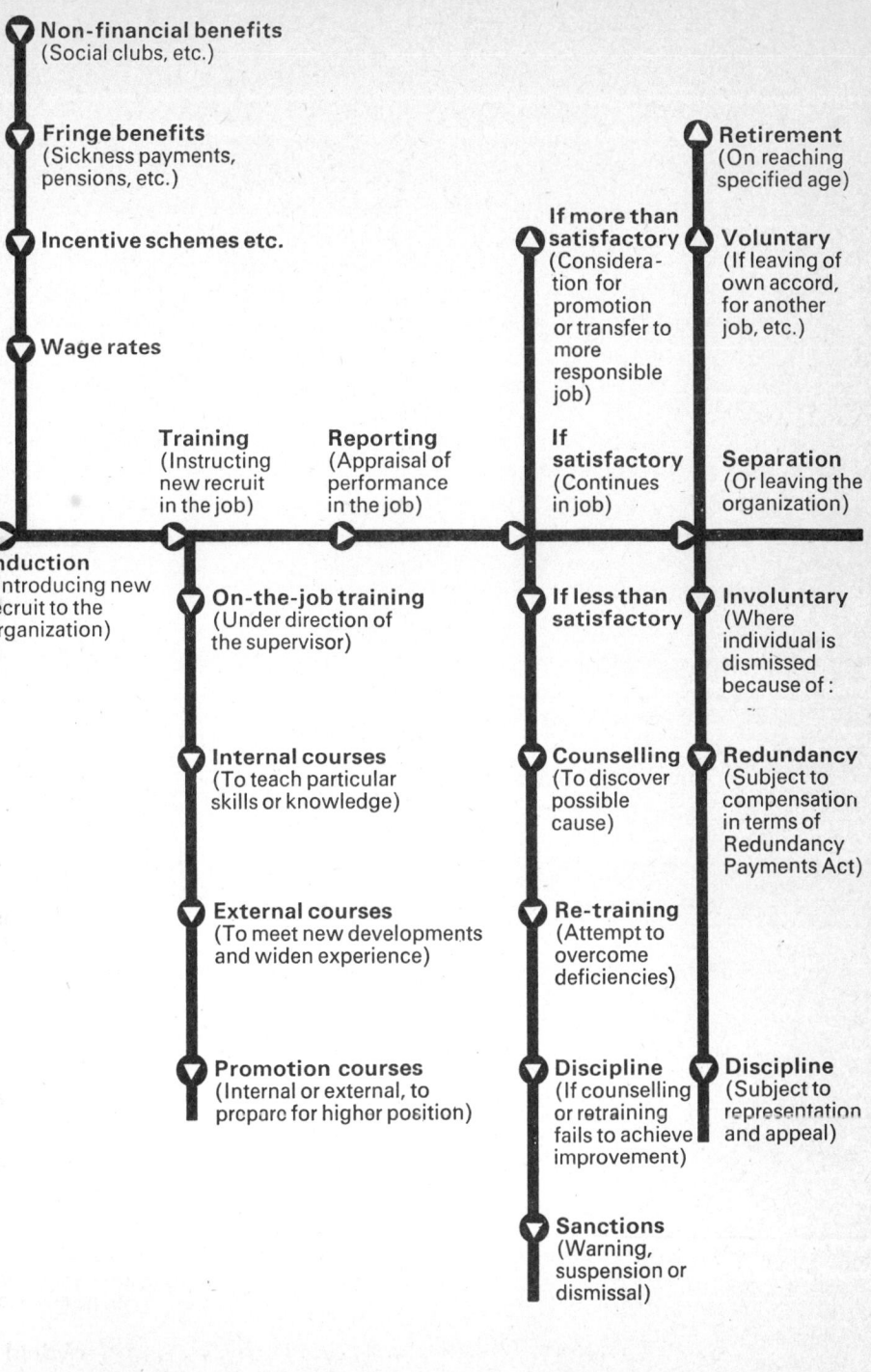

Non-financial benefits
(Social clubs, etc.)

Fringe benefits
(Sickness payments,
pensions, etc.)

Incentive schemes etc.

Wage rates

Training
(Instructing
new recruit
in the job)

Reporting
(Appraisal of
performance
in the job)

**If more than
satisfactory**
(Considera-
tion for
promotion
or transfer to
more
responsible
job)

**If
satisfactory**
(Continues
in job)

Retirement
(On reaching
specified age)

Voluntary
(If leaving of
own accord,
for another
job, etc.)

Separation
(Or leaving the
organization)

Induction
(Introducing new
recruit to the
organization)

On-the-job training
(Under direction of
the supervisor)

**If less than
satisfactory**

Involuntary
(Where
individual is
dismissed
because of :

Internal courses
(To teach particular
skills or knowledge)

Counselling
(To discover
possible
cause)

Redundancy
(Subject to
compensation
in terms of
Redundancy
Payments Act)

External courses
(To meet new developments
and widen experience)

Re-training
(Attempt to
overcome
deficiencies)

Promotion courses
(Internal or external, to
prepare for higher position)

Discipline
(If counselling
or retraining
fails to achieve
improvement)

Discipline
(Subject to
representation
and appeal)

Sanctions
(Warning,
suspension or
dismissal)

new skills and technical knowledge which will be required is thus necessary.

People change also. They develop and they grow older. Some leave for other jobs, and some retire when they reach the specified age. Some get fed up with the jobs they are in, and look for promotion, or at least for a change. To expect that the personnel of an organization will remain static for the next 12 months is to close one's eyes to reality. The manpower plan should provide for all these changes. It should provide for succession if higher-level jobs become vacant. And it should provide a career structure for the ambitious people who want to make something of themselves in their working life.

Recruitment

The manpower plan will show the vacancies expected over the next few weeks. The next step is to find applicants for these vacancies. And we shall want more than one applicant for each vacancy. If we hope to make any selection, we must have people to select from. Selection means picking and choosing. And if there is only one applicant for a job, we cannot pick and choose. We must take what we get and hope for the best. Recruitment, or the provision of a suitable number of applicants, is thus a task for the personnel department.

In a full-employment situation it is a difficult task. So long as there were queues of unemployed, the Department of Employment and Productivity's Employment Exchanges were a source of recruitment and usually produced a number of suitable applicants. Those days, however, are gone, and no one wants to see them back. Nowadays the Employment Exchanges often have more vacancies on their books than they have registered unemployed. Unfortunately, also, many of those who have been unemployed for any length of time are, in fact, unemployable. For one reason or another, they are unable to stick at a job, and they drift in and out every few weeks. One result of this is to give the impression that the Employment Exchange is not much use as a source of recruitment. This is not entirely just, for when they have enough applicants on their books they perform an invaluable service.

The Employment Exchanges have special registers also. One of these is for professional and executive staff, which can be a source of applicants for higher-level jobs. Another is the Register of Disabled Persons. Each company is required by law to employ 3% of these; the Department's Disablement Rehabilitation Officers (DROs) do their best to fit handicapped people into jobs they can cope with. If the job does not require standing up all day, for example, they may find someone with a leg disability who may be suitable for it.

A second source of recruitment is press advertising. This is almost a study in itself, for different papers and periodicals circulate among different types of people. If you want a fitter, for example, it would be rather a waste of money to advertise in *The Times*. The local evening paper might catch the attention of suitable applicants for a job like this. But the advertisement would have to be sufficiently attractive to make it seem worth while for someone already in a job to consider changing. Press advertising is expensive and a careful watch is necessary to make sure that the company is getting value, in suitable applicants, for the money it spends.

There are various employment agencies which can form a valuable source for different kinds of staff. Some of these specialize in office staff, and can produce temporary employees to meet an emergency. Various professional institutions perform this kind of service for their members. It is the task of the personnel department to know which of these will produce suitable applicants for certain types of job.

A notice at the gate lets it be known in the district that there are vacancies in the company. But one source which can be of the greatest value is recommendations from existing employees. When the labour situation is very tight indeed, some firms have gone so far as to offer a cash bonus to anyone who introduces a satisfactory new employee. And this raises an important point in connection with recruitment. If the firm is known to be a good place to work, it will have an advantage. Existing employees will be willing to introduce their friends. Word will get round the district and people in other firms who want a change will be anxious to apply. Every company has a public image in the locality. This will make its recruitment problems easier if it is a favourable one—or more difficult if it is unfavourable.

Job Analysis

Once we have the applicants lined up, we can start selecting the ones we want. But in this chapter so far we haven't given any thought to the kind of person we *do* want. This is a serious omission, so we must go back on our tracks for a bit to consider the question. In the first place, we must know a lot more about the job we want the new starter to carry out.

This involves a procedure known as *job analysis*. There are various ways of setting about it. If the job is a straightforward repetitive one, we simply need to watch what the operator does. We can then record his actions and, if necessary, time them. Work study experts are trained to do this in detail and they can finish up with a schedule covering every movement the operator makes. F. W. Taylor was one of the earliest practitioners of this, and he was followed by Frank Gilbreth, the inventor of the Therblig (Gilbreth spelt backwards). This is a kind of shorthand for recording hand movements —'reach', 'search', 'grasp', 'position', 'assemble', and so on. When a job is studied by a work study specialist, he finishes up with a moment-to-moment list of the movements involved. He also has the timings of these movements. He knows more about the job, in fact, than the chap who actually does it.

This doesn't make the work study expert very popular. Nobody likes other people looking over his shoulder all day. And few people will believe that the job they've been doing for months, or even years, can ever be understood by someone who only looks at it for a couple of hours. There is a certain amount of sense in this, because there is sometimes a knack in jobs that can be missed by the observer. For these, and for other reasons connected with piecework rates, there is sometimes conflict when the time-and-motion expert appears on the factory floor.

When a work study expert—or even an amateur with some idea of the principles—looks at a job in this way it is usually obvious that there are things that could be improved. Sometimes the layout could be changed round to make tools and equipment easier to reach. Sometimes unnecessary movements could be cut out. Both hands could be used at the same time, and so on. It is often surprising how wasteful 'the way we've always done it' turns out to be.

Ergonomics

A further development of this is the science of *ergonomics*. This is based on a study of the human body, which, from this point of view, is a sensory-motor mechanism. That is to say, it takes in information through the senses, and it makes movements by means of its muscles and limbs. In the sort of job we are thinking of, the operator is receiving signals through his senses—the movements and position of the machine or the material he is working on. He is working out the meaning of these signals, and responding to them by movements of his hands and feet which control the process. An example familiar to everyone is driving a motor vehicle. The driver sees the road and the traffic in front of him, and also behind in his mirror. He turns the wheel, presses the accelerator or the brake, and changes gear, to control the speed and direction of his own vehicle.

The ergonomist is concerned in the first place with how the operator receives information. If the driver had to look over his right shoulder to see the approaching traffic; over his left to see what was behind; under his arm to see the speedometer; and between his legs to see the red light of the ammeter; driving would be a difficult, not to say a dangerous, task. This, of course, is an exaggeration. But there are jobs in industry where the information is pretty difficult to take in—gauges set above or below eye level, with too-small figures on them; machines where it's impossible to see the working parts; assemblies where you can't feel how the parts fit together. The ergonomist's task is to redesign the job or the machine so that the operator can easily take in the information he needs, and interpret it quickly and correctly. Eye-level dials with clear figures and pointers; beams of light directed on the cutting tool; ridges and corners that can be felt clicking into place—modifications like these have been introduced into various jobs by the ergonomists.

Their second task is to make the movements required as simple and convenient as possible. Harking back for a moment to the motor vehicle: if the driver had to lean out and put both hands and all his weight on a handbrake to slow it down, driving would be a dangerous business. This would be an awkward movement, demanding a disproportionate amount of effort. Instead of this, in a modern vehicle, we have a footbrake placed at a level where a comparatively small amount of pressure produces the result. The ergonomist is concerned with designing controls to be as convenient as possible for the limb movements of the average human being. This means the positioning of handles, pedals, and other controls so that they are easy to reach and can be manipulated with the minimum of effort.

What Supervision Involves

Although the work study expert or the ergonomist can deal with operators' jobs, things get a bit more complicated above this level. An operator's job is essentially a task. As we have said, it involves taking in information, making judgments on it, and responding by muscular movements to achieve the desired results. But supervisory and management jobs are social roles. That is to say, they put the individual into relationships with other people. And the management of these relationships plays a large part in success in this type of job. For this reason, the study of these higher-level jobs presents more difficult problems.

One way to approach these jobs is to ask the people concerned about how they spend their time. This has been done with a number of supervisors with the following results. First, 109 supervisors were asked which kind of task took up most of their time. This was done on a sort of ranking method, the supervisors noting which task took up most time, and which came next. Two points were awarded for a first mention and one for a second. When the points were added together and worked out as percentages of the total, the following picture emerged:

Planning tasks, allocating duties to operators, arranging their work ahead, arranging for things to be available to them, etc.   **40%**

Technical tasks, advising operators on methods and helping them out in difficulties with their work   **21%**

Operator tasks, connected directly with the work they were in charge of   **18%**

Inspection tasks, checking up to see that jobs had been properly done   **11%**

Upward contact, receiving information and instructions from those above, passing information upwards, etc.   **5%**

Personnel tasks, sorting out difficulties with people, discipline, dealing with awkward people, etc.   **5%**

Studies like these cannot always be depended on, however. They place too much reliance on human memory and judgment. When a supervisor answers, he may be influenced by the fact that last week he had to spend more time than usual on a certain task. Or again, he may be giving the answers that he thinks he ought to give—over-estimating the time he spent on planning the work of his operators, and playing down the time that he spends on the tasks his operators ought to be doing themselves.

Another approach is to ask people which part of the job gives them most worry. This was put to the 109 supervisors mentioned above, and the order of the various tasks changed considerably. This became:

Personnel tasks	**27%**
Planning tasks	**24%**
Operator tasks	**19%**
Technical tasks	**13%**
Inspection tasks	**12%**
Upward contact	**5%**

The difference here is that personnel tasks have jumped from the bottom of the first table to the top of this one. Sorting out difficulties with people, dealing with awkward people, etc., may not actually take up a lot of time throughout the day. But the amount of worry connected with these tasks is apparently much greater than the actual time involved.

Such studies help to give some indication of the pressures of the job. Here again, however, they may be affected by what happened yesterday. And again people may be giving the answers they think are expected of them.

What seems a more satisfactory method is to ask a supervisor or manager to keep a diary of what he does during working hours. In this, he notes down what he does from moment to moment throughout the day. If several supervisors can be persuaded to do this honestly and in detail, valuable information can be obtained. This can be studied and broken down under various headings which will tell us a great deal about what these jobs involve.

There is still another approach, which is known as *activity sampling*. This simply means that someone walks through the place at regular or irregular intervals and notes what the people being studied are doing at the time. At first glance it may appear unfair. For if a supervisor happens to be taking the first chance in weeks to have a quiet drag at a cigarette, he may be marked down under the heading 'not usefully occupied'. But the more observations that are taken, the more likely it is that a realistic picture of his job will appear. This, of course, takes us into statistical theory, for the reliability of the sample depends on its size as well as on other factors. But as a means of analysing non-operator jobs it has been used on a number of occasions.

Job Description

We have already discussed organizations, and pointed out how they should be made up of fixed areas of responsibility. It is equally obvious that within these areas there should be a series of clearly defined jobs. Each individual should know what he's there for, and what's required of him. Thus, what follows from our job analysis should be a clear *job description*.

Quite often, when one starts trying to define jobs more exactly one runs into trouble. 'We've always got along all right,' people say. 'What's he poking his nose in for? What's it matter who does what, so long as it's done? Just a waste of time, all this is!' In a traditional establishment, this may be all very well. People know each other and have worked together for a long time. They share responsibility and help each other out. Even here, however, there can be trouble when things go wrong. Everyone can put up a good story that it wasn't his fault. But we are becoming less and less concerned with traditional organizations. Our industry is changing rapidly as new processes and new products appear. Supervisory management is becoming less and less a matter of taking charge of a well-established department, and more and more the management of change. Most supervisors will find themselves appointed to take charge of new developments probably several times in their working life. And it is their success in making these work efficiently that plays the major part in their further promotion.

When the job analyses have been done, therefore, we should finish up with a series of job descriptions. These set out in detail what is expected of the individual concerned, and serve several purposes. They form the basis for management by objectives. They also let the person in the job know what is expected of him. Accurate job descriptions should be on file in the personnel department. At the same time, the supervisory manager should have done some thinking on these lines. After all, he is the source of the information on which most job descriptions must be based.

The following headings cover most of what is required.

Title of job. This is essential as a means of identification. It may sound a bit comic to talk of a 'sagger-maker's bottom-knocker' and so on. But without some sort of title, no one knows which job we're talking about. It is an advantage, of course, if the title can be made as meaningful as possible.

Duties and responsibilities. These can be laid out in greater or less detail, as the situation requires. Where highly developed work study departments exist, they can include a complete breakdown of the job, with the relevant timings. In other cases, they can set out the standards to be achieved in more general terms.

Skills and knowledge required. Where the job can be learned by anyone in a short time, this will not matter. Where, however, the job cannot be done without certain qualifications in skill and experience, these can be stated.

Working conditions. Whether the job is carried on in hot or other trying circumstances; whether it is in a normal factory or office environment; whether it involves working alone, or with a group of others; all such matters can be listed under this heading.

Economic conditions. Rates of pay, bonus or overtime rates, holidays, sick payments, or other fringe benefits can be listed here.

SUMMARY

1 *What do we mean by manpower planning?*

Manpower planning is the attempt to forecast the numbers and types of personnel that will be required in an organization. This will depend on the replacements necessary to maintain the existing staff. It will also be affected by any technological or organizational developments which may call for special skills or qualifications in the future. An effective manpower plan will anticipate these, and will also take into consideration the careers which the organization offers to its employees.

2 *What recruitment problems are presented by present-day conditions?*

Recruitment means the provision of applicants from among whom to select. Unless there are more applicants than vacancies, no selection is possible. Full employment, when Department of Employment and Productivity Employment Exchanges have more vacancies than unemployed, presents the main problem. Press advertising, agencies, and recommendations from existing employees are possible sources of applicants, but these will usually be in jobs already, and will only be attracted by a vacancy which offers added inducements.

3 *What is the purpose of job analysis?*

Job analysis is the process by which a job can be studied and its content recorded. Work study specialists have their methods of observation which are useful for repetitive manual jobs. Jobs which are social roles rather than tasks can be studied by asking people to record their activities, to say which involve most time and worry, or by activity sampling.

4 *What does the term 'ergonomics' mean?*

When a manual job is studied systematically, it is usually apparent that the method could be improved. Ergonomics is the study of jobs in terms of human capacities and limitations. It is concerned with the design of equipment so that the necessary information is easy to take in, through the layout and placing of dials, etc., and so that the movements required of the operator are as simple as possible, by the convenient placing of pedals, levers, etc.

5 *What is a job description?*

The result of an effective job analysis will be a job description, which sets out the content of the job in detail. The following headings cover most of the factors:

Title of the job
Duties and responsibilities
Skills and knowledge required
Working conditions
Economic conditions

CHAPTER 6 Job Specification

Once the job has been studied and an accurate description drawn up, we come to the next question. What sort of chap is going to do this job properly? What sort of chap is going to reach the standards we have set? What sort of chap is going to meet the demands it makes? This brings us to the job specification.

There can be some confusion over words here, for these terms are not always used in the same way. To recapitulate for a moment, we are using the terms:

Job Analysis to describe the process of studying the job, its methods and equipment. This leads on to:

Job Description, or an account, in greater or less detail, of the actual content of the job. From this we derive:

Job Specification, which sets out the personal qualities required in the man or woman who will do the job to the standards set.

Thus, the job description describes a job, whereas the job specification describes a human being. This presents us with a problem. There are an awful lot of human beings in the world, and each one is quite different from the rest. Each one is an individual, with his own particular make-up or pattern of personality. And when we try to classify human beings into types, we usually run into difficulties. For every one who fits into our classification, there will be at least one exception. In addition to this, human beings can change from day to day. The chap who is helpful and easy to deal with on Friday may be awkward and pig-headed on Monday. It all depends on how he's feeling at the time. And this again may depend on how he's got on with other people over the weekend. Human beings are not isolated entities. They have to live together and enter into relationships with other human beings.

Faced with all this, how do we set about describing the sort of person we want? Well, the starting point is to take one thing at a time. If we concentrate on one personal quality, or one aspect of human beings, we shall find that things simplify themselves quite a lot. For any one quality, the differences between people follow a certain pattern. If we take something that is easily measured—height, for example—we shall find that a lot of men are around the average, say 5 feet 6 inches to 5 feet 9 inches. We shall find rather fewer above the average or below the average. And we shall find fewer still very much above or very much below the average. This can be shown diagrammatically in what is known as the *normal curve of distribution* (Fig. 9).

This normal curve of distribution is a useful thing to know about. It crops up in quite a lot of unexpected places. If we toss four pennies, for example, it will predict the chances of how they will fall. In quality control, it helps to tell us the number of samples that should be checked to ensure a certain standard of quality. A great

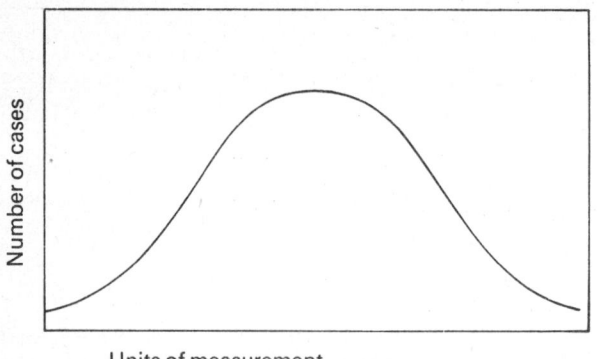

Units of measurement

FIG. 9. *The normal curve of distribution*

deal of statistical theory centres round this curve. For the practical man, however, it simply means that most of the cases fall into the middle of the range, round about an average. As we go above this average, the number of cases tails off until it dwindles to nothing. As we go below the average, the same thing happens. And when we look at human beings from any one point of view, we shall find that they are normally distributed.

The next question that arises, of course, is how many points of view do we need to look at? We suggest that the following five will be sufficient for an adequate job specification. When a job—or a human being—has been studied from these five aspects, very little has been left out.

Impact on Others
There are questions of health and fitness—whether the job requires an exceptionally strong man, or one who can stand up to very trying conditions. In the same way, there are certain physical

disabilities which can rule a man out without further consideration. All these matters are the job of the doctor, not of the supervisor or the personnel department. If any question arises about a person's health or fitness, medical advice should be sought. It is a waste of time for the layman to poke his nose in.

Some jobs, however, may require a good deal of contact with other people. Supervisory and other management jobs involve a lot of this, and bring up the question of how other people react to the individual. People differ in their dress and appearance, in their speech and manner, and in their self-confidence in talking to others. You may think that all these are superficial qualities, and that they are less important than certain other attributes—whether the chap knows the job, and whether he's a hard worker. You may also think that because a chap's a smooth talker, this doesn't guarantee that he's any good in other ways. You could be quite right at that. But you could also be overlooking an important point.

Appearance, speech, and manner may be only on the surface. But these are the qualities to which other people react. Thus, if anyone is below the average from this point of view—if he's rough in manner, uncouth in speech, and if his clothes look as though they've come out of the dustbin—other people aren't so likely to enjoy his company. They may even try to keep out of his way and avoid having anything to do with him. In certain jobs—particularly supervisory management jobs—this would be a handicap.

In laying out a job specification, therefore, this is the first thing to be considered. Does the job involve dealing with other people? If so, we want someone above the average in his impact on others, for success in such jobs depends on getting the right reaction. Take the salesman's job, for example. A salesman may know all about his product, he may be keen and hard-working; but unless he calls out a favourable reaction from his customers, he won't be much good as a salesman. This is a condition of success in the job. And in any other job which involves dealing with people, the same thing will apply.

There are other jobs, of course, where impact on others doesn't matter so much. On the factory floor, so long as the other chaps don't object to his presence, below-average appearance, speech, and manner make no difference. Then again, there are jobs where a man works away by himself all day, and has no contact with anyone. The important thing is to look at the job from this point of view by itself, and to consider its requirements separately. We can then say that anyone below a certain standard in his impact on others will have little chance of success.

Qualifications

The second point of view is the simplest of the lot. This concerns the skill and knowledge the individual must have before he can tackle the job. And standards of skill and knowledge can be laid down in black and white. If the job requires a professional engineer we could lay down an A.M.I. Mech. E. as a minimum standard. If it involves specialized knowledge of heat-treatment equipment, we can say we want 2 years' experience in that field. Similarly with other jobs.

It sometimes helps to break down this heading into three sub-headings. These are:

(a) *General education*, which can be expressed in examination results—G.C.E. 'O' level or 'A' level, etc.
(b) *Specialist training*, in terms of Ordinary National or Higher National Certificate, membership of professional institutions, etc.
(c) *Work experience*, measured in the time spent in different kinds and levels of job.

We are not for a moment suggesting that this aspect of the job specification is not important. It is very important indeed, and in many cases, without a certain standard of qualifications, no one could be considered for a job. But under this heading we have definite standards in examination results, acceptance by professional bodies, and years of experience. These make it much easier to lay down specific requirements for any job. Under some of our other headings, things are not quite so definite.

Brains and Abilities

There are some jobs which can present a fresh problem every morning. And there are others where the same routine has to be carried out day after day. In the first type, we need someone who can think quickly, understand new situations, and produce new ideas about how to cope with them. In the second type, the quick thinker would soon get bored and fed up. In the routine jobs, someone with a slower mind might be quite happy.

This aspect of the job specification opens up the question of intelligence testing, which we shall deal with later on. All that concerns us at the moment is whether the job needs 'brains' in the sense that it involves quick thinking. If so, we need someone who is above the average from this point of view. If it presents few new problems and merely involves carrying out a repetitive task, we can go lower down the scale.

There are, however, other aptitudes that can be called into play. Manual dexterity, or 'neat fingers'; mechanical aptitude, the ability to see how things fit together—some jobs depend to a great extent on these. People with these particular aptitudes pick up such jobs very quickly and easily. Those who lack them take much longer to train, and often fail to reach the required standard. Such aptitudes can be measured by appropriate tests and minimum standards can be set, below which the chances of success are slight.

Brains and abilities are all very well. But it is the use an individual makes of these that really matters. This brings us to our next point of view.

Motivation

Some jobs need hard work and concentration. Others can be done quite easily when one is thinking of something else. Thus, the amount of effort required can vary from job to job. This is perhaps the aspect that calls for most study, from two points of view. To put someone who lacks the necessary drive and determination into a job where success depends on these qualities can have serious consequences—to the individual as well as to the organization. On the other hand, to put an ambitious and hard-working young man into a job which allows no scope for these qualities is to invite trouble. The young man will quickly become frustrated and will either leave to look for a better job; or he will find ways of working off his dissatisfaction that will make him a nuisance in the working group.

Here again we can think of averages. There are jobs which demand a certain amount of concentration but not a lot of initiative. Jobs where, so long as the chap does what's been set out for him, he earns his money quite satisfactorily. There are also jobs where the organization says, in effect: 'We're putting you in charge of this particular area of our activities. We're expecting these results from it, and we're relying on you to achieve these results. We're putting certain services at your disposal, but we're leaving it to you to make use of these services. Anything that stands in the way of the results we want, we're expecting you to deal with. You'll be on your own for a large part of the day. You'll have to plan your own time, and decide which things you're going to do first. If you achieve the results, you'll get the credit. But if you don't, we're not interested in the reasons for failure. It's your job, and your responsibility.' This is the kind of situation which calls for someone above the average in the qualities we are considering under this heading.

We shall be discussing motivation in greater detail later on in the

book. It is one of the most important aspects of the human being—
at least so far as working life is concerned. At this stage, however, we
need only raise the question of how much drive, initiative, and self-
direction is called for in the job specification.

Adjustment

This aspect of the job is concerned with the amount of emotional
pressure it involves. If the chap can come in in the morning and get
through the day without being worried or pushed around, the
standard will be pretty low. But if he is constantly being chased by
other people, called on for quick decisions, and having to take the rap
when things go wrong, the standard required will be above the
average. Once again, each job must be considered separately from
this point of view. When this is done, differences will quickly be seen.

Sometimes the equipment or the material can be a cause of
worry. Wrong decisions in this kind of job can result in serious losses,
and we need a steady sort of chap to make them. But more often
people are the main source of pressure. For people can raise more
problems than any sort of plant. Practical problems always have an
answer, though this may call for specialized knowledge or experience.
Moreover, once a practical problem has been solved, it stays solved.
But problems with people do not always have an answer. Worse still,
when we think we have solved them one way, they crop up again in
another form. Pressures at work usually have their origin in other
human beings. Thus, where a job involves responsibility for other
people, the job specification must lay down a high standard from this
point of view.

Everyone can stand a certain amount of pressure. But everyone reaches a point where he blows up. This is the breaking-point,
where he becomes incapable of rational behaviour. Some people
have low breaking-points, while others can stand greater degrees
of stress. The supervisory manager must have a high breaking-point
if he is to stand up to the pressures of his job.

Job Specification

Once a job has been studied in the manner described in the
previous chapter, a job specification can be drawn up for the kind of
person required to carry it out successfully. The following example
may help to make this more realistic. We have taken a first-line
supervisor's job in an assembly department, and laid out a description
on the lines suggested. From this we have derived a job specification,
using the five headings outlined above.

EXAMPLE OF JOB DESCRIPTION

1 Title of Job
First-line supervisor (foreman) No. 3 Assembly Section.

2 Area of Immediate Responsibility
No. 3. Assembly Section consisting of:
(a) *Five service hands* whose training and experience enables them to do any job in the section. They can relieve or temporarily replace operators, and can be made responsible for the day-to-day running of parts of the section.
(b) *Twenty-five operators* who are semi-skilled and can each carry out an individual, work-studied task to a set level of performance.

The first-line supervisor has overall responsibility for the running of the section. This can be subdivided into:

(a) *Output.* The target being 95% of the theoretically possible production from the plant. He is responsible for achieving this level of machine utilization, while at the same time meeting delivery requirements as they arise.
(b) *Quality*. The target being no more than 2% rejects. He is responsible for foreseeing any variations in quality and taking appropriate steps to put them right.
(c) *Equipment.* He is responsible for noting any faults in the running of the plant and taking steps to have them rectified.
(d) *Costs.* A budget for direct wages and material and a rate of overhead recovery have been set for the section. The first-line supervisor is responsible for keeping within this budget.
(e) *Personnel.* He is responsible for the 30 people under his charge. This includes not only the quantity and quality of their output, but also their training, safety, and their general well-being and morale. Communication with them should pass in the first place through him.

3 Position in the Organization (See Fig. 10)
(a) *The line organization.* He is immediately responsible to the second-line supervisor (general foreman) in charge of the assembly department (Mr Black). Overall responsibility for the department lies with him, and the first-line supervisor is one of his immediate subordinates. Above the second-line supervisor is the manager of the components division, who in turn is responsible to the production manager.
(b) *Links with the functional organization*
    (i) *Production control department:* which lays down weekly programmes of output for each section of the assembly department. These may require modification to meet delivery

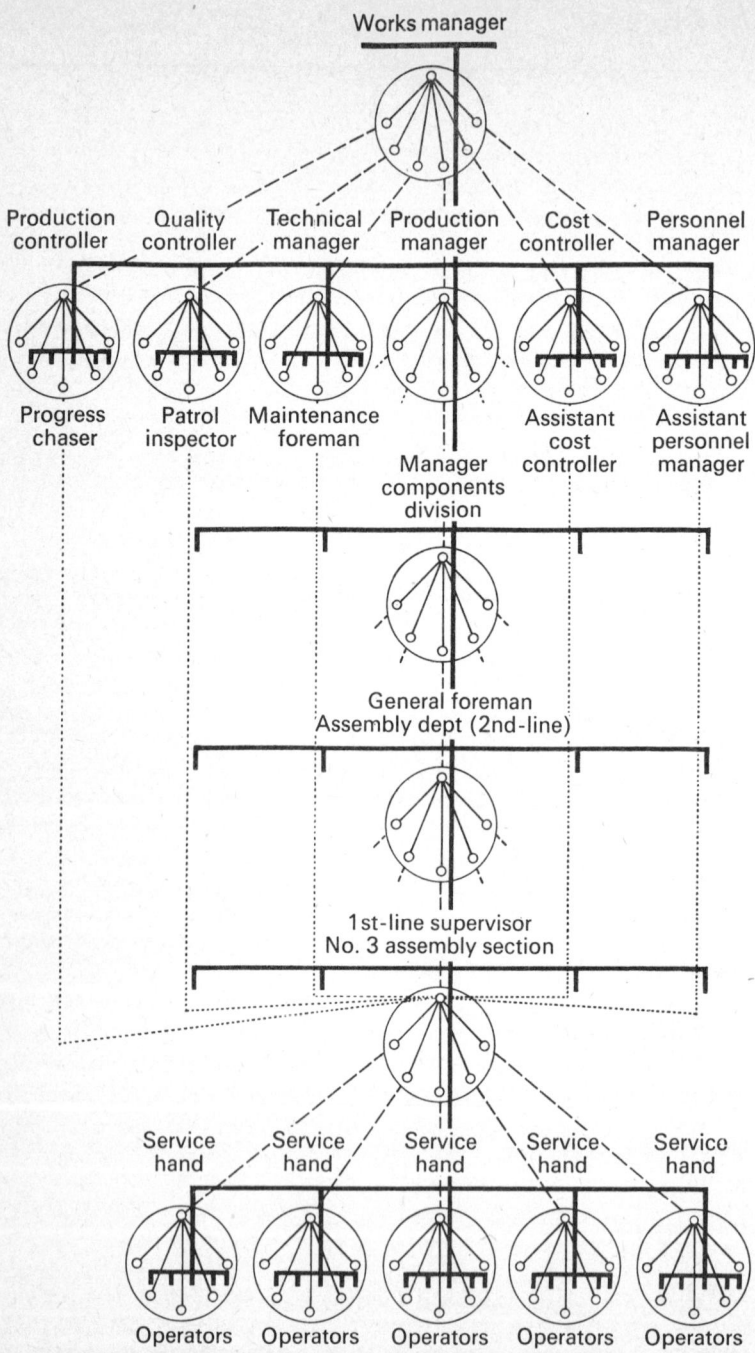

FIG. 10. *Chart to illustrate job description of first-line supervisor, No. 3 assembly section*

requirements. This department is also responsible for ensuring that the necessary parts and components are forthcoming. His contact with this department will be the progress chaser (Mr White).

(ii) *Quality control department:* which lays down standards of quality and is responsible for all gauges and other methods of measurement. His contact with this department will be the patrol inspector (Mr Brown).

(iii) *Maintenance department:* which is responsible for the running of all plant and equipment. In the event of any faults or breakdowns, his contact will be the maintenance foreman (Mr Green).

(iv) *Cost Control:* He will receive a periodic statement of the direct labour and material used in his section. Any variations from the budgeted figures will be discussed with his immediate superior (Mr Black) and the assistant cost controller (Mr Silver).

(v) *Personnel department:* which is responsible for replacing any operators who leave, and to whom any queries on wages, training, safety, disciplinary sanctions, promotions, or transfers should be addressed. His contact with this department will be the assistant personnel manager (Mr Scarlet).

4 Skills and Knowledge Required

Knowledge of an assembly department will be an essential requirement, though not necessarily within this particular section. Anyone from within the assembly department would be considered adequately qualified from this point of view, as would anyone with similar experience in another firm. No formal engineering qualifications are necessary.

Some formal qualifications in industrial administration are, however, necessary. Without these, it is very doubtful whether an applicant would understand his position in the organization.

5 Working Conditions

Normal factory conditions prevail, with no excessive exposure to heat or cold. There are no fumes or other elements in the atmosphere. No physical strain beyond being on his feet most of the day. Normal factory hours. Desk and telephone screened off in one corner of the section.

6 Economic Conditions

Staff status with salary on Grade VI level. (As the actual amount will vary, it may be misleading to put an exact figure here. It should, however, provide a satisfactory differential above the earnings of the operators under his charge.) Sick pay on normal staff rates. Three weeks' holiday on full salary. Membership of the staff pension fund.

This should serve as an illustration of the job description. In practice, of course, it should grow out of the actual organization of the company. Any attempt to make one up runs the risk of artificiality. However, the above will serve to bring out the main points.

Now we turn to the job specification, or the type of man who will successfully fill this position. Using the five headings outlined above, this works out as follows.

Impact on others. This job involves continuous contact with other people. Its occupant must be in close touch with his service hands and through them with his operators. He must maintain friendly relations with the supervisors in charge of other sections in the department, and with the representatives of the functional departments with whom he is in touch. He must be on confidential terms with the second-line supervisor above him, and he must on occasion be able to talk confidently to representatives of higher levels in the organization. From all these, he must be able to draw out the kind of reaction called for by the situation.

To do all this, he must be able to express himself adequately in conversation with a wide range of people. In some cases, he must show a certain forcefulness to get his point across. In others, tact and persuasiveness will be called for. He must be sensitive to the reactions of others and must be able to tread lightly when there is a chance of calling out antagonism. At the same time, he must be able to face up to hostility when this cannot be avoided. He must have a reserve of self-confidence to deal with all the interpersonal situations that may arise. And he must have enough self-control to be able to adapt his manner to these situations. From all these points of view, he must be above average.

So far as appearance is concerned, it will be an advantage if he is reasonably neat and tidy in his turnout. Insufficient attention to these details would have an unfortunate effect on his initial impact.

From the health point of view, there are no special requirements beyond normal fitness. As he is to become a member of the pension scheme, however, a medical examination would probably be called for.

Qualifications. A suitable applicant is likely to be in his middle twenties and will have attended a secondary modern or comprehensive school. Some evidence of achievement at school such as possession of a Certificate of Secondary Education would be desirable but higher educational qualifications, such as G.C.E. 'O' level, are not essential. It might be advisable to check that the applicant can express himself adequately in writing, either by asking him to write a report or in some other way.

Specialist training in supervisory management would be essential. The successful applicant must produce evidence, in the form of examination results or a certificate, that he has completed a course of formal training. Without this, it is very unlikely that he would be able to take his place effectively in the organization.

Work experience should include at least 1 year on assembly work of a similar nature. In addition to this he should have experience of other factory work, preferably with some minor responsibility.

Brains and abilities. Though he is in charge of routine work, the first-line supervisor has a far from routine job. He goes into action when the routine breaks down or threatens to do so. He must thus have the kind of mind which can deal with new situations; can foresee difficulties before they happen; and can produce the new ideas required to cope with these exceptions. No special aptitudes are called for, and if tests are used a minimum of the average for the general population on a test of general intelligence would be set.

Motivation. It is in this area that the qualities most essential to success will be found. It is likely that most of the operators under the first-line supervisor's charge will be of average motivation. That is to say, they will think: 'I come here to earn a living. I'm prepared to work at whatever job I'm given, so long as it's properly laid out, and so long as they provide the tools and material I need. I don't feel that it's my job to deal with anything that goes wrong, there should be somebody else to look after that. If they want me to work, then it's their business to see that I have everything I need for the job.' This is the level of motivation one can expect on a routine, semi-skilled job. Its limitations are obvious. But if one is realistic about human beings at work, it must be accepted.

If this section is to work effectively, it is again obvious that the first-line supervisor's motivation must take on where that of the operators leaves off. When they ask: 'Well, what do we do now?' he is the one who must supply the answer. He must provide the extra drive and determination which overcomes the obstacles. He provides the initiative to deal with new situations as they arise. And he foresees what is going to happen next, and works out the necessary arrangements. In everyday speech, he is on the ball.

From all this, it follows that the first-line supervisor must be above the average in the qualities we are calling motivation. It also follows that these are the qualities on which success in the job mainly depends. He may be well spoken and well qualified; he may have the right experience and plenty of brains; but unless he has the necessary 'go' or drive, he will not be successful in the job. This will show in all sorts of little ways. Things will not get done; plans will not work out; obstacles will not be overcome. There may be a perfectly good reason for every one of these. But the fundamental reason will be a lack of motivation in the first-line supervisor.

Adjustment. This again is a job which involves pressure. The first-line supervisor is at everybody's beck and call. His superiors will be after him to see that production keeps going. The functional departments will be worrying him about their particular responsibilities. His service hands will be bringing news about difficulties on the job. And the operators will want him to listen to their grouses and complaints. He will be constantly under the temptation to fly off the handle and shout: 'How the hell do you expect me to deal with that now? I can't do everything at once!' This is the breaking point, which everybody reaches sooner or later, when the pressure has become more than they can cope with.

People have different breaking points. Some begin to shout the odds after only a small amount of pressure, while others remain calm and collected even when things go wrong in a big way. This is where the different levels of adjustment show themselves in practice. And it is again obvious that the first-line supervisor must be above the average from this point of view.

This again is one of the qualities on which success in the job largely depends. The first-line supervisor is the focal point through which a great deal of essential communication must pass. The effective working of the organization depends upon this. Communication takes place between people, and continual contact with people is a major source of pressure. Unless he can take this pressure, and unless he can remain cool and collected when others are clamouring for his attention, he will not be fulfilling his essential role in the organization. This will show up in various ways. From the organization's point of view the most serious will be that he will be by-passed. When people find that they cannot get the answer from him, they will go to someone else. From his own point of view, the danger is that he will break down under the strain.

SUMMARY

1 *What does the term 'job specification' mean?*

A job specification sets out the personal qualities which an individual needs if he is to carry out the job successfully. It describes a human being, not a job.

2 *What are the headings under which personal qualities can most conveniently be laid out?*

    (a) Impact on others
    (b) Qualifications
    (c) Brains and abilities
    (d) Motivation
    (e) Adjustment

3 *Do people differ in each of these qualities?*

Certainly. For each quality there will be an average, to which the largest proportion of cases conform. There will be fewer cases above the average, and still fewer very much above. There will likewise be fewer cases below the average, and still fewer very much below. This arrangement of differences is illustrated by the bell-shaped normal curve of distribution.

4 *What is the significance of impact on others?*

This is the aspect of the individual to which other people react; his appearance, speech, manner, and skill in dealing with interpersonal situations. There are some jobs in which this aspect plays a major part in success—sales jobs, for example. In any job where contact with other people is important, this aspect should be considered.

5 *What is the significance of qualifications?*

This covers everything the individual knows and can be subdivided into:

    (a) General education
    (b) Specialist training
    (c) Work experience

As these can usually be expressed in objective standards—examination results, certificates, or years in a particular kind of job—this aspect presents few problems. It is important, however, that the demands of a job should be laid out as accurately as possible in these terms.

6 *What is the significance of brains and abilities?*

These reflect the individual's 'quickness in the uptake' and his aptitude for picking up certain types of work. Tests have been devised which are helpful in estimating these qualities, and are useful in setting minimum standards. One must always remember, however, that the possession of ability does not guarantee that it will be put effectively to use.

7 *What is the significance of motivation?*

This covers the targets an individual sets himself, his consistency in following them up, his initiative in overcoming obstacles, and his effectiveness in action. It is the heading under which 'success' qualities are most frequently found. Some jobs demand only average standards from this point of view, the ability to carry out a routine task which makes few demands. Others, particularly supervisory jobs, demand higher standards, for the supervisor's above-average motivation must make up for the limitations of the people he supervises.

8 *What is the significance of personal adjustment?*

This covers the individual's ability to stand up to emotional pressure, and in most jobs it means the pressures of dealing with other people. An average here is the person who can fit in with others but cannot take responsibility. Jobs like those of supervisory managers, which involve continuous responsibility, would drive the average person over his breaking point. They thus demand above-average standards.

CHAPTER 7

The New Recruit

Recruitment, job analysis, and preliminary selection will normally be the responsibility of the personnel department. The supervisory manager will not come into the picture until the stage of final acceptance. He should, however, have a grasp of all the steps in the process —partly because of his overall responsibility for collaborating intelligently with functional departments, and partly because this final stage is the most important. This is where the decision is taken. And, no matter how much preliminary work has been done, it is good personnel practice to leave the decision on final acceptance in the hands of the person who has to take direct responsibility for the new starter's work. The person who takes this final decision must therefore understand the steps that lead up to it.

Let us recapitulate these steps from the point of view of the supervisory manager.

Notification of Vacancy

When one of the employees in his section hands in his notice, the supervisory manager will put in a request for a replacement. If this is simply a matter of bringing his numbers up to the authorized level, this request will go through as a matter of routine. The personnel department will start the process of looking for a replacement. If, however, the staffing of the section is under review, one man's leaving may provide the opportunity for a painless reduction in numbers. It may therefore be decided not to replace that leaver, but to carry on with one less. On the other hand, even though no one is leaving, the stepping up of the work load in the section may make an increase in staff necessary. Thus, a vacancy may be authorized in addition to the existing staff.

This is where the supervisory manager comes up against the manpower plan. Provided that it has been properly worked out, his requirements in personnel should be authorized without argument. If he has to argue the toss and fight for extra men to meet his commitments, then there is something wrong with the manpower planning. If, on the other hand, he tries to hang on to people when they are not really needed for productive work in his section, then he is not collaborating intelligently. The ideal to be aimed at is that his work load and his personnel should be properly in balance.

Interviewing the Applicant

The various stages of recruitment and preliminary selection will then be carried out by the personnel staff. In due course, the supervisory manager will get a telephone call from them. Someone will say: 'About that vacancy you've got for an assembler. There's a chap on his way down to see you. He worked for Brown and Jones for a couple of years in the assembly department. Then he moved to Smith and Robinson for 18 months on a similar sort of job. He wants to come here because it's nearer home for him. He seems a reasonable sort of chap—looks you in the eye and all that. His experience seems in line with what we want, and he seems bright enough to pick the job up fairly quickly. He's held his last two jobs for a fair time, so he must be a reasonably hard worker. And he seems to get on all right with people, so I don't think he's likely to be a trouble-maker. Have a look at him, will you? Show him the job, and then give me a ring and tell me what you think.'

The reader will have noticed that this phone call has given a quick summary of the applicant from the five points of view mentioned above. To recapitulate:

'He seems a reasonable sort of chap'   . IMPACT ON OTHERS
'His experience seems in line with what we want'
                                                          QUALIFICATIONS
'He seems bright enough to pick up the job'
                                                     BRAINS AND ABILITIES
'He must be a reasonably hard worker'   MOTIVATION
'He seems to get on all right with people'   ADJUSTMENT

This is the result of the preliminary interview in the personnel department, carried out by someone with some specialist training. We cannot go into detail here, but the general idea is that the more you find out about what an individual has done in the past, the more you know about his personal qualities. These personal qualities show themselves in what he makes of the various situations presented to him. Thus, if someone has had seven jobs in the last six months; if in each of these he claims to have been victimized and 'picked on'; if he complains about the supervision or the working conditions in one after the other; then there is almost certainly something wrong with his motivation and adjustment. Nothing is perfect in human affairs, but it is not very likely that he would be presented with seven bad supervisors in seven lousy jobs one after the other. A much more simple explanation is that there is something wrong with him that has made him fail to fit in with the job. Interviews in the personnel department should find out as much as possible about what the applicant has done in the past. On this factual information, an assessment can be made which will determine whether he should be sent on down to the supervisor.

Armed with this preliminary information, the supervisor can carry out his own interview. This will have three aims:

(a) To find out a bit more about the applicant in order to decide about his suitability.
(b) To let him find out as much as he wants about the job and the company.
(c) To establish an easy relationship with him.

Of these, the most immediately important is the easy relationship. Without this he won't 'open up', and you won't be able to find out anything about him. Moreover, you want him to get a reasonably pleasant impression of the place. Not only will this make it more likely that he'll accept the job—other things being equal—if it's offered to him. It will also make him come in expecting to be treated decently, and not with his guard up, ready to defend himself against you.

The easiest way to establish the kind of relationship you want is to listen. It's amazing how quickly people open up when they find they've got an interested and sympathetic listener. Thus, when you start asking him about his last job, show that you're taking in what he says by plenty of 'Oh's' and 'Ah's' and 'Is that so's?'. Similarly, when you show him the job pay plenty of attention to his questions, and answer them in a way that calls out further questions. Make it your business to see that he does most of the talking, while you do most of the listening.

Assessing the applicant. Underneath your interested and sympathetic manner, however, you should be doing some hard thinking, because you've got to reach a decision about whether to take him on or not. And this will depend on your making up your mind about the five requirements set out above.

The first one, *impact on others*, needn't delay you for long. This job doesn't involve much contact with people outside the other chaps in the section. So long as you think they'll accept him, he'll be all right from this point of view. The only snag that may arise is when the applicant is coloured, or when he comes from another country. In principle, we don't discriminate on grounds of race, colour, or creed. In practice, however, some working groups have strong feelings about non-British applicants being introduced into them.

The supervisor will know about these feelings, even though he may not share them. And he may be presented with some difficult decisions over applicants whom he knows may upset the section if they are taken on.

The second aspect, *qualifications*, will need a bit of thought. The supervisor should find out as much as he can about the applicant's previous jobs—exactly what types of assembly he has worked on; what tools he used; and what standards of accuracy he was working to. He can then compare these with the job for which he is being considered. If they match up, then from this point of view the applicant will be acceptable. If they don't match up, the supervisor must consider whether a little training will bring him up to standard. This will turn his attention to the other points.

Does the applicant have enough *brains* to pick up the job fairly quickly? This will depend on whether he sees the point of questions, and responds intelligently, or whether he seems unduly slow on the uptake. It will also depend on whether his last job demanded any brains, even though its content was different. We must not overstate the case, for assembly work does not call for an intellectual genius. And if the chap is too bright, there will be a danger that he will get bored and frustrated by the monotony of the job. Nevertheless there are some pretty stupid people around. And if you get landed with one of these, he'll take up far too much of your time in showing him the job and teaching him how to do it.

Then again, there is his *motivation*. Does he seem a hard-working type? Information about this will come from his previous jobs, about which, by this time, you should have gathered some information. You will probably know something about the firms for which he has worked too. If he has kept up to the pace of an efficient and well-organized firm for a reasonable time, then he is probably all right from this point of view. But if he has been the first to be stood off when things got a bit slack, you may have doubts about his motivation. When you are considering this aspect, you should be careful to stick to facts. Anyone can shoot a line about how keen he is to get on in life; to work hard in an efficient and well-known firm; and to qualify for a better job. But unless this is backed up by a record of progress at work, it should never be taken too seriously.

Finally, does he seem a *well-adjusted*, stable, and reliable person? Here again, his work record will provide useful information. If he has been entrusted with a little extra responsibility and has stood up to this successfully, this is the sort of evidence you want. On the other hand, if he seems to have been shifted around for no particular reason, the people he worked with may have found him a bit difficult. You may get some more evidence from the way he talks about the people he has worked with and the firms he has been employed by. If he can discuss these in reasonable terms, he's probably all right. But if he's got a catalogue of hard-luck stories and grouses about being done down, you may be justified in having some doubts.

It may sound as though we're expecting rather a lot from a 20-minute chat with someone you've never seen before. If you know what you're doing, however, it's surprising how much you can learn in a short time. Get the applicant talking—that's the starting point. Then listen to what he says, and consider him from each of the five points of view in turn. You won't be right every time, of course. But if you use your loaf and delay your decision until you've considered each point separately, you'll be right much oftener than you're wrong. And you'll make very few really bad mistakes.

Information about the job. While all this is going on, you'll be showing the applicant the job, and telling him about the conditions. It is important to be absolutely frank about this, and to go out of your way to make sure that he understands what will be expected of him. Few things create more bad feeling than a new starter who can say: 'This job isn't what you led me to expect. You gave me to understand that I would be doing so-and-so. Now you're asking me to do something quite different. I've been led up the garden, and I'm not going to forget it.' From that point on the new starter will have a chip on his shoulder, and may become the centre of trouble. To avoid this, you should take a great deal of care to show applicants what will be expected of them, and to tell them about conditions, methods of payment, earnings, and so on. All these will be available in a properly worked-out job description. This is another reason why the supervisory manager should be in the picture about these matters.

Acceptance of the Applicant

When he has collected all the information available and weighed it up, the supervisory manager can get on the telephone again to the personnel staff. If he thinks that the applicant measures up to the job, he can simply say: 'O.K. I think he's all right. Will you take him on and arrange for him to start on Monday?' If, however, it is not as simple as this, then the following kind of conversation can take place.

'I'm not too happy about that chap you sent down. His experience isn't much use to us, and he doesn't seem too bright to me.'

'Don't you think his time at Brown and Jones would be a help?

He was there for 2 years, and he seems to have earned his money all right.'

'Yes, but he was on very simple stuff. Didn't have to use any tools. We'd have to train him in our jigs and power tools more or less from scratch.'

'I see. Does he strike you as a steady sort of chap?'

'Oh, yes, I think he's all right from that point of view. It's the time we'd need to train him that's worrying me.'

'Do you think he'll take long to pick it up?'

'Well, that's the point. He doesn't strike me as too bright. What are the chances of getting anyone better?'

'I'm afraid they're pretty dim. Things are a bit tight just now. We've only had three applicants for this job, and he's the only one that seemed worth sending down to you.'

'What were the others like?'

'One was a real drifter. Four jobs in the last 3 months. The other had just been sacked from Universal for what he called "a bit of trouble with the foreman". I think he took a poke at him. He looked as though he easily could have done. Gave me a mouthful of abuse when I told him we'd no vacancy that would suit him.'

'Is that so? Well, I've got enough trouble on my hands without having to go in for self-defence. Any chance of others turning up?'

'It's a bit doubtful. We've had this job open for over a week.'

'And I've got to have someone on Monday, or we'll be in a right mess. I think we'd better take him on and do the best we can to train him. Once he's picked the job up, I think he'll be all right.'

'O.K. I'll get on with it.'

This illustrates the various points that have to be weighed up— the need to fill the vacancy quickly; the state of the labour market; the time required to train the new starter; the chances of his turning out a satisfactory worker. Such a decision requires judgment. It can never be reduced to a cut-and-dried procedure. One should never give the impression that selection is a routine matter of shoving pegs into holes.

Personnel Department Routines

When a decision has been reached to accept the applicant, a number of routines must be carried out. The personnel department will want details for their records, and for passing on to the wages office. Insurance cards must be obtained and the Contracts of Employment Act adhered to. This requires that each new employee must be shown his conditions of service, and must sign a form to indicate that he accepts them. There may be other matters, such as clock numbers, membership of sick clubs, pension funds, etc.

We need not concern ourselves with the details of employee records, for the supervisory manager will have little to do with them directly. He should, however, have some idea of the use that can be made of these records. There are various analyses that can be made from time to time which can provide very useful information. Some examples follow.

Absenteeism. This can be measured by the percentage who fail to report for work each day. This percentage can be broken down into figures relating to voluntary absence, where the individual has stayed away for no good reason, and involuntary absence, where a worker has been unable to come in through illness, accident, or other unavoidable reasons. Such figures may show that certain causes seem to be cropping up with disturbing frequency. Or they may show up differences between departments. In such cases, further enquiries will be called for in order to do something about it.

Accidents. Absence figures will call attention to safety, for any absence over 3 days due to an accident has to be reported. Once again, a study of the figures will trigger off an attempt to do something about the causes.

Timekeeping. This can also be treated in the same manner. Figures may show that punctuality is better or worse in some sections, among certain age groups or types of employee.

Labour turnover. This is simply the number of leavers over a year, expressed as a percentage of the total personnel. It can be very useful as an indication of the stability of the company's employees. If, for example, the labour turnover index were zero, this would mean that no one had left or been replaced throughout the year. If, on the other hand, the index were 100%, this would indicate that a number equivalent to the total personnel had left and been replaced.

A high labour turnover can be an expensive business, for recruitment and training of new starters costs money. It is therefore in the firm's interest to keep it as low as possible, as will be obvious to the supervisory manager. After all, he is the person who has to cope with all the interruptions to production which arise when people leave and new starters have to be trained.

Various factors, however, can affect a company's labour turnover. The level of employment in the area; competition among employers for workers; the company's wages and conditions in relation to others in the area; these and other matters can push it up or down.

Comparisons between departments within a company can also be revealing. If it is shown that of two similar sections one has a labour turnover of 25%, while the other across the passage has a turnover of 75%, then one would want to know why. If the conditions are the same, what is wrong in the second department? Is it the supervision? In a case like this, it would be advisable for the supervisor to do a little hard thinking about why people are leaving his section. There is, of course, a further difficulty. When asked why they're leaving a job, people don't always give the real reason. It is much easier to say that there's better money at so-and-so's, than to tell the foreman that you don't like his face.

Labour turnover figures are necessary in manpower planning. They indicate the number of replacements that will be needed to keep the personnel at the present level. A figure of 25%, for example, indicates that one-quarter of the existing staff are likely to leave and be replaced over the next 12 months. This will involve the necessary arrangements for recruitment, selection, and training. Within a section of twenty-five, this will mean six or seven new starters. As has been said, there are various factors which affect the level of labour turnover. In the industrial areas generally, a labour turnover of 25% is reasonably low. Some companies reach figures much higher than this. Management has to accept, therefore, that there will be a pretty considerable movement of personnel under present-day conditions.

Wastage rates. These indicate how long people are staying with the company. If, for example, 50% of leavers have less than 1 month's service, then an alarming proportion are packing up the job soon after their appointment. This reflects badly on the company and its working conditions. Moreover, it calls attention to a considerable source of loss. Most new starters only begin to be productive after they have been in the job for some time. If, for example, they leave before they have completed their training, they represent a source of considerable expense which has not been offset by any production. Wastage rates call attention to this sort of loss. And, once again, comparisons between departments can be extremely illuminating.

Induction

The first day in a new job can be rather a worrying experience. You don't know where anything is. You don't know who the people around you are. You're not sure exactly what you have to do. And you don't know when anything's going to happen. All this can produce a very uncertain frame of mind, in which small things take on a disproportionate importance, and where you feel very exposed and on the spot.

As time goes on, of course, things sort themselves out. You get used to the place and the people. And the little things that worried you on your first day fall into place as you gain confidence. Confidence, incidentally, is rather an odd thing. There is confidence in yourself. And there is confidence in other people. The one grows out of the other. If you know what to expect of the people round about you, and if you can rely on them to be considerate and helpful, you'll feel quite sure of yourself. But if you feel that the people around you are just waiting for a chance to do you down, you'll feel very exposed and on the defensive. And you'll be ready to take a chance on getting in first and taking a smack at them, before they start on you.

This is more or less how anyone feels on his first day in a new job. And the sooner he gets through this period of initial strangeness the better for everyone. If the new starter can settle down quickly, he'll feel more at home and be easier to deal with. He'll also get down to his job or his training and become productive in shorter time. How, then, can we speed up this settling-in process?

The essential element is for the new starter to form a relationship with someone in the organization. For, when he finds that there is someone he can talk to and ask questions of, he has found a fixed point in the strange situation. This someone ought to be the supervisory manager, or perhaps the semi-supervisor in whose charge he has been placed. In either case, it ought to be someone who has a responsible position in the organization, for this first point of contact will represent the organization to him, and it is important that it should be represented in the proper terms.

When the new starter arrives in the department, therefore, the supervisor must find time to take him under his wing. He must show him the essential things he needs to know. A checklist of these might be handy, on something like the following lines:

Clocking-in arrangements
Cloakrooms or lockers for outdoor clothing
Toilet and washing facilities
Time of morning tea break and how arranged
Time of lunch break, canteen location, and arrangements
Time of afternoon tea break and how arranged
Time of finishing work and any routines involved

This should ensure that he knows what happens throughout the day and where the essential conveniences are to be found. It should also ensure that he feels there is someone in the place who takes an interest in him, and to whom he can refer in case of any doubt or difficulty.

The next step will be to get him started on the job. And this is where induction may shade into training, which we deal with in the next chapter. It will still be necessary to introduce him to the group of which he will be a working member, and to put him under the charge of the semi-supervisor who should be the central figure in it. When he gets started on the job or training, it will still be advisable to find opportunities to chat to him several times during the first day and the first week. The ideal to aim at is that, if he has anything on his mind, the supervisory manager will be the natural person for him to talk to. How and when this should be done is up to the supervisory manager. One point which should not be missed, however, is the first week's wage packet. Money is important to all of us. And if the new starter has any queries about how much he has been paid, the supervisory manager should be on the spot to answer them.

The induction process is important in determining the person with whom the new starter has formed his most significant relationship. If this is the official representative of the organization—the supervisory manager—then he is likely to feel that it is taking some interest in him as a person. From this some feeling of identification will follow naturally. Future communication with him will thus be normal and easy. But if his first significant relationship is with someone other than his supervisor, all sorts of difficulties may be anticipated. The friends on whom he feels he can rely will not be representatives of the formal organization. They may, in fact, be in opposition to it. His integration into the unofficial group will thus follow naturally. And from then on the supervisory manager may well appear a hostile figure, representing an organization which is out to exploit him and do him down. It will seem sensible to protect himself against this by banding together with the rest of the chaps. In this way, the organizational structure at the level where the work is done will become less and less effective. Communication and control will slip into unofficial hands. And the supervisory manager's job will become progressively more difficult. It is thus worth while to find the time to make sure that the induction of a new starter is properly done during the first morning.

SUMMARY

1 *What steps should the supervisor take when a vacancy arises in his section?*

He should notify the personnel department. If the manpower plan does not envisage any change in the numbers authorized for his section, arrangements for a replacement should automatically be put in hand. If, however, the plan provides for a reduction in numbers, this normal wastage provides the opportunity to cut down the strength of the section.

2 *How should the supervisory manager interview an applicant?*

He should first be provided with an outline of his background by the personnel department. Then, by encouraging him to open up in conversation, he should find out more about the applicant's last job. He should then make up his mind about the five aspects—impact on others, qualifications, brains, motivation, and adjustment—in terms of the particular job. If he considers that the applicant measures up to the requirements on all of these, he should tell the personnel department that he is willing to accept him. If, however, he has any doubts, he should discuss them with the personnel department, to weigh up the chances of finding a more suitable applicant.

3 *What should an applicant be told about the job he is applying for?*

He should be shown the job and the working conditions. He should be told about the hours, wages, and probable earnings. He should, in fact, be told everything possible in the time available, and be encouraged to ask questions. The danger to keep in mind is that when he starts the job, he can complain that he was not given a proper picture of what was expected of him.

4 *What does the supervisory manager need to know about employment records?*

He needs to know very little about the routine of record keeping. He should, however, appreciate the significance of periodic analyses of absenteeism, accidents, time keeping, labour turnover, and wastage rates. Figures of these for his own section should be available; he should also know how these compare with the organization as a whole.

5 *What do we mean by induction and what is its significance?*

Induction is the process of introducing a new starter to the job and the organization, and helping him to settle in. It covers the day-to-day arrangements for clocking in, cloakroom arrangements, times of breaks, etc., as well as the actual routine of the job. Induction is important in determining the new starter's impressions of the firm and his attitude towards it. It is also important in deciding the relationships he forms on his first day. The most significant of these relationships should always be with his immediate supervisor.

Training is what you do to other people. Learning is what they do themselves. This is not only a distinction in terms of words. It draws attention to a very real difference between two processes—learning and teaching. Ideally, they should link up together, for unless the trainee has learned something the trainer is wasting his time. The measure of success in training is how much and how quickly the trainee has learnt—not how hard the trainer has worked, nor the amount of impressive apparatus he has collected.

Before we tackle the actual methods of training, we must spend a moment on some underlying principles. The first of these concerns the trainee's willingness to learn.

Motivation of the Trainee

Human beings do things because they see some point in them. They will only put forth effort when they think it is likely to be rewarded. These rewards are not always measured in money terms. They can also depend upon social approval and prestige.

When you are concerned with a training situation, therefore, you should start by putting yourself in the trainee's place. You should then ask yourself: 'As a trainee, what do I expect to get out of this?' If he is simply being trained in a limited skill, then his reward is to get on the job and begin earning money. If he is being trained in a wider range of skills, the reward may include an element of status and enhanced competence. If he is being trained for a social role, it may include a feeling of confidence and increased awareness. Whatever the situation, the trainer should try to ensure that this reward is never lost sight of, and that the trainee is kept continually aware that he is making progress towards it.

The role of a trainee is not a particularly attractive one. If a chap is being trained, then by definition he knows less than other people. He is in a position of inferiority, and no one likes to put up with this for a moment longer than he can help. There is always some underlying hostility in a training situation. One occasionally meets this in management courses. Some people take the idea of being sent on a course as an insult to their dignity. 'What,' they say to themselves, 'do they think I don't know my job? Do they imagine that I'll benefit by sitting listening to some clever young bighead who thinks he knows it all? Someone who's never been inside our factory and who knows nothing about our industry? Well, I suppose I've got to go if they say so. But if I get a chance to take these people down a peg, I'll make the most of it.'

This kind of attitude is unfortunate from two points of view. On the one hand, our industrial development depends upon our managers and supervisors continually getting new ideas. And on the other, the individual's personal development depends on continually widening his range of experience. When anyone gets to the stage where he thinks he has nothing more to learn, he has come to a full stop as a person. And as nothing ever stands still, he will soon start slipping back.

Anyone concerned with training must be aware of all this, and must take it into consideration in his methods of training. It can be turned to good account, however. All the steps in a training programme should be seen to lead towards the result desired by the trainee. If he can see himself working towards his goal, his motivation will be stimulated. On the other hand, if he thinks: 'They keep me messing around on little things I can't see any point in. I don't seem to be getting anywhere in this place,' then his motivation will be undirected and frittered away. He will either resign himself to this pointless messing around, or he will leave for another job with a bit more future to it.

A Training Programme

The best way to offset the frustrations of the training situation is to plan a series of steps. This makes it easy for the trainee to see that he's getting somewhere.

Each of these steps should make sense in itself. That is to say, it should contain enough material to make it a recognizable part of the job. On the other hand, it should be understandable in the time available. The aim should be that, at the end of each lesson, the trainee can say to himself: 'Well, I've got that part straight. I know where I stand with it. Now I'm ready to go ahead with the next bit.'

Each step should also conclude with some sort of check to ensure that the trainee has grasped the material in it. One way of making this check is to give the trainee a trial run against the clock: if he carries out the required number of operations in the specified time, he can be considered competent in that step. Another way is to give the trainee a series of questions: if he answers these correctly, he has understood the content of that step. This is one of the key elements in programmed learning, often presented by a teaching machine. For instance, at the end of each step, the programme may present the trainee with a series of questions for which are several suggested answers shown. If he selects the right answer, the learner goes on to the next step. If he selects the wrong answer, he goes back to do that step over again.

This method breaks down what has to be learned into a training programme. Each step in the programme makes up a lesson. The content of each lesson should be understandable by the trainee in the time available. And the test at the end should serve several purposes. In the first place, it should be a check that he has grasped the content of that lesson. In the second, it should provide him with an immediate target at which he can aim. And in the third place, the feeling of achievement he gets from having passed the test should stimulate his motivation. These are the basic principles that should be applied in any training project.

In some organizations, the first-line supervisor is responsible for training his operators. This places him in a difficult position, for to put what we have said above into practice will take up a lot of time and attention. He may thus be tempted to put the new starter along with an experienced operator and let him 'pick the job up' from him. This, of course, is quite the most unsatisfactory method of training. Firstly, there is no guarantee that the experienced operator is willing to pay much attention to the trainee. Nor can we be sure that he has any idea of how to make the training effective. His own methods of working may not be the most efficient, for he probably picked them up himself by 'sitting next to Nellie' in the first place. His attitudes to the job and the organization may also be very different from those we want passed on to the new starter. This is the kind of training that we should be trying to get rid of as soon as we can. We should make every effort to replace it with something that will not only cut down training time, but will also pass on better methods and attitudes. This should start from the first half-day at work.

Where an organization is big enough to justify a separate training school or department, these difficulties disappear. New starters can then be given a properly planned course which makes full use of the processes outlined above. In many cases these training departments recover their costs several times over by cutting down the time taken for a new starter to reach piecework speed. They are, however, likely to be found only in the larger firms. In many cases, training will still have to be done in the production departments, and will remain the responsibility of the first-line supervisor. Even here, however, improvements can be made, and the services of a training specialist may be useful.

Within a production department, someone can be appointed as a trainer. This can be a kind of semi-supervisory post, but care should be taken to select the right kind of person. He should make the kind of impact on others that will gain the new starter's confidence. He should also have the qualifications, motivation, and adjustment required for this added responsibility. There are plenty of people on the factory floor who measure up to this, and they can be given a little specialist training. They can be shown how to break jobs down into manageable elements, each of which can be practised to the standards required. And they can be shown how to build up these elements into the complete job. They can look after the new starter for the first few days, and act as his guide, philosopher, and friend until he is fully into the swing of the job.

Apprentice, Supervisory, and Management Training

So far we have been dealing mainly with operator training, as this will usually be the supervisor's main concern. There are, of course, other forms of training which we can quickly summarize. Apprentice training is important because on it depends our future supply of skilled men. The skills needed by industry, however, are changing. Hand craftsmanship and traditional experience are becoming less valuable, while the importance of theoretical knowledge and the ability to understand new technological developments is increasing. 'Serving his time' for 5 years, during which the apprentice picked up his craft from experienced men, is falling into disrepute. Modern apprentice training is carried on in apprentice schools on a planned programme, and by day-release or sandwich courses in technical colleges which lead to a recognized qualification. The supervision of apprentices now rests in most cases with someone specially appointed for the purpose.

The training of specialists may be done partly within the organization itself. An increasing part, however, is being played by outside bodies. For many years industrial consultants have organized courses for work study engineers. Technical colleges have developed similar courses and have also provided instruction in other management techniques. As these techniques develop, courses appear in production control, industrial relations, value analysis, data processing, and so on. We cannot do more than mention these, for new developments are constantly making their appearance. The value of these courses, however, can vary according to the degree of control exercised over the standards.

One way of looking at the training of supervisors and managers in industry is to consider it as a longer-term method of management. When any change has to be made which is of more than day-to-day significance, some form of training is necessary to introduce the people concerned to the new method, product, or material. If this matter is neglected, then the results will be what one might expect— botched-up learning with a half-understood idea of the new development which misses some of the essential points. If, on the other hand, a well-organized course can be found which will cover the subject systematically, then the people concerned will end up with a proper grasp of the new development, and what it is likely to demand of them. With the rapid progress in management techniques which is taking place, one might suggest that every supervisor or manager should have time off every year, or at most 2 years, to attend some kind of course bearing on his job. This would have the added benefit of keeping his mind open and counteracting the 'we've always done it this way' outlook.

Reporting or Appraisal

The principle of management by objectives can be applied to all aspects of an organization's working. Standards can be set, and reports called for on whether these standards are being met. For the personnel function we have standards already available in the job specifications. All we need, therefore, is a series of reports on whether individuals are matching up to these standards.

It is good practice to have a regular reporting or appraisal system in an organization. This can begin, say, a month after the new starter has joined the firm. Another report can be called for at 3 months, and another at 6 months. After this, all staff can be reported on at 12-monthly intervals. The form of the report can be under the five headings already set out. The standards can be in terms of the levels called for by the job. Thus, an annual report on the first-line supervisor appointed to the job described in Chapter 5 might take the following form.

Most appraisals are done quarterly

Impact on others. Deals effectively with the people under his charge and obtains suitable responses from them. Can make his point in discussion with the people above him and obtain satisfactory collaboration from functional departments. Expresses himself competently; self-confident, while at the same time sensitive to the reactions of others. From this point of view, well up to the standards required.

Qualifications. Satisfactory understanding of the technical working of his section, with sufficient grasp of specialist functions to collaborate intelligently with these departments. Is pursuing further studies with

a view to obtaining formal qualifications in supervisory management.
Brains. Never stumped by a new situation. Well up to standard from
this point of view.
Motivation. Has met all demands in terms of output, quality, etc.
Extremely hard-working and conscientious. Shows initiative in the
right places and can summon reserves of drive and energy when
required. Very satisfactory under this heading.
Adjustment. Remains calm and collected under pressure, and is not
provoked into outbursts of bad temper. Can deal effectively with
awkward situations and remain in complete control of himself.
Meets demands of the various social roles in which the job places
him.

A reporting system of this nature would provide a yearly 'audit'
of the personnel of an organization. Provided the reports were satisfactory—namely, that the individuals were meeting the demands of
the various job specifications—no further action would be called for.
There would be, however, cases where further consideration would
be necessary. These would be, on the one hand, where the individual
was reported on as failing to live up to the job specification, and on
the other, where he was more than meeting these demands. We shall
deal with the latter case first, as it presents fewer problems of
principle.

Few organizations are burdened with too many people for the
top-level jobs. Many find themselves short of suitable candidates for
promotion. On the other hand, there is a comparatively limited
proportion of people with above-average motivation and adjustment
who want to get ahead in their working life. From both these points
of view, therefore, it is important to spot those with potentialities for
promotion as quickly as possible, and to give them the opportunities
of which they can take advantage. When a report indicates that
anyone is more than meeting the requirements of a job, he should be
considered for further training and possible promotion. In this way,
the organization will make the maximum use of its resources in
personnel, while at the same time it will provide the career structure
which will encourage people with the right personal qualities to stay
with the firm.

When, on the other hand, the report is less than satisfactory, the
first step should be to determine where the individual is falling short.
Here again, the five headings come into play. We can consider
whether his *impact on others* is failing to call out the sort of reactions
which the job requires. We can decide whether his knowledge or
experience is falling short (*qualifications*) or whether he is not quick

enough at grasping the problems presented to him (*brains*). We can look at his *motivation* and decide whether his inadequate performance is due to lack of drive and energy. And we can consider whether his *adjustment* is of too low a level to stand up to the stresses of the job.

Once we have decided where the individual is falling short, we have to face the question: 'What do we do about it?' Here we are presented with a series of steps which should be considered one at a time.

Counselling

This is an American term which has a slightly formal ring about it. The actual process, however, is perfectly simple. It just means that when a report is discussed between the person making it and the person reported upon—and this should be the standard practice—the former says something like: 'Look, old chap, I've got to put a report in on you for the past year, and I'm afraid I'm not giving you exactly full marks on all counts.' The other will then say: 'Oh, where have I gone wrong?' or something like this, and then a discussion can start.

This may not always be an easy situation to handle, but nevertheless it is part of the responsibility of anyone in charge of other people at work. If it goes well, it should enable the supervisory manager to point out his subordinate's weaknesses in such a way that the latter accepts the criticisms in the spirit they are offered. One must guard against the danger of becoming starry-eyed and thinking that subordinates will always agree with the criticisms and, choking back a sob, promise to do better. All the same, people have a right to know where they stand. And even though they may not like it at the time, it may clear the air if an unfavourable report is frankly discussed with them—particularly if the person making the report has a good enough level of adjustment to keep the situation under control, and not let it degenerate into an acrimonious argument.

Retraining

One result of a counselling interview may be a decision that further training is necessary. This will obviously be the case if the shortcomings concern qualifications. Depending on the arrangements in the firm, an individual can be given further instruction by his immediate supervisor, by an internal training course, or by going on an outside course. If one or other of these proves effective and the next report is satisfactory, then the situation will have been dealt with successfully.

Discipline

When, after an unsatisfactory report followed by a counselling interview, there is no improvement, then a disciplinary problem is presented. There is a kind of borderline here, which the supervisory manager must recognize. There are cases where he may think: 'Well, so-and-so is not ideal in the job, but he does his best and, by and large, he's producing the results we want.' Such a case could be classified as just satisfactory and no further action taken. There are other cases where he may think: 'So-and-so's not up to the standard we need. I've talked to him about it, but he's making no effort to improve.' A case like this calls for action, and moves into the category of discipline.

Every organization ought to have an established disciplinary procedure which involves a number of clearly defined steps. These are as follows.

1 Warning. This is where the individual concerned is told that he is falling short, and formally warned that if he does not improve, action will be taken. Such an interview is quite different from the counselling sessions described above, and this should be made quite clear. Warnings should be recorded, so that the individual cannot later protest that he was not told. It may be advisable for such warnings to take place in front of a witness, possibly for the individual to have a representative present, and for the record to be noted by the personnel department. If a formal warning is disregarded, then the organization is justified in taking the next step and applying *sanctions*. These may take one or other of the following forms.

2 Monetary sanctions. In some cases it has been the custom to deal with persistent late-coming by the stoppage of $\frac{1}{4}$ hour's wages. In other cases, merit bonuses, or other benefits for which the individual has previously qualified, can be withdrawn. Care must be taken to ensure that statutory regulations are not infringed, as these lay down conditions covering such stoppages.

3 Suspension. This involves telling the individual that he cannot report for work for one or more days. It has the effect of depriving him of his wages for the time specified.

4 Dismissal. This is the final sanction in industrial employment and is, in fact, the last resort. It can have a serious effect, for when the individual applies for another job, it will constitute a black mark on his record. With the present standard of worker representation, dismissals—and indeed all disciplinary sanctions—must be handled with the greatest care. Unless the firm has an absolutely watertight case, the consequences can be serious. Fellow workers or their representatives may consider that justice has not been done, and may threaten action in the form of a strike. In most cases an appeal procedure will enable the individual to put his case. If this succeeds the dismissal notice may have to be withdrawn, with serious consequences for the organization. Nothing shakes the basis of discipline more than an attempted dismissal which does not come off. In view of this, it is usually impracticable to leave the authority to dismiss with the supervisory manager. In most cases it rests with higher management, usually represented by the personnel department. The only exceptions are flagrant breaches of discipline such as fighting, threats of violence, and the like.

SUMMARY

1 *Why is it important to study the motivation in a training programme?*

Because no one will ever make any effort unless he sees some point in it. Unless the trainee feels that what he is being taught is worth while, he will not apply himself to learning it. In any training situation, care should be taken to ensure that its objectives are clear and that the trainee understands how he will benefit by attaining them.

2 *What are the main points to bear in mind when organizing a training programme?*

Any training programme should be organized in a series of steps. Each of these should form a recognizable part of the job, which can be understood in the time available. Each should be practised until a given standard has been attained. At the conclusion of each step there should be a check or test to ensure that the trainee has reached the standard aimed at.

3 *How can the training of operators best be planned?*

If the organization is large enough, a separate training school can be set up. Each trainee can be passed through a programme which has been carefully planned in detail. Where the size of the organization does not justify this, operator training must be carried out on the job under control of the supervisory manager. Wherever possible, however, trainers should be appointed to look after new starters. These can be given instruction in training methods and can apply sound principles to the actual training situation.

4 *What methods are available for training skilled workers?*

The traditional method of training skilled workers was by apprenticeship, during which the young person picked up his skills and experience by serving his time under a craftsman. As the skills in demand now call for a greater knowledge of the relevant theories, apprentice training is moving towards a more systematic introduction to the technology of the industry and a planned programme of instruction in its practical application.

5 *How can the training of specialists, supervisors, and managers best be dealt with?*

As management techniques become more sophisticated, specialists in these techniques must be trained by outside bodies. Universities, technical colleges, consultants, and professional institutions provide courses, some of which lead to qualifications of a recognized standard. In addition to these, introductory courses for line managers and supervisors are also necessary. The effectiveness of these techniques in day-to-day working usually depends on the student's appreciation of their practical value.

6 *What should be done when a person is reported on as either: (a) more than meeting the demands of the job; (b) failing to meet the demands of the job?*

In the case of (a) he should be considered for further training with a view to promotion.

In the case of (b) a counselling interview should be given to clarify where he is falling short, and further action, in the form of retraining, considered in the hope that this will overcome the shortcomings. If this is unsuccessful, then he should either be transferred to another job, or dealt with as a disciplinary problem.

7 *What are the essential steps in a disciplinary procedure?*

(a) *Formal warning*, which should be witnessed and recorded, and where the individual concerned may be represented if he so desires. If this is ineffective, then *sanctions* must be applied. These may be:

(b) *Monetary sanctions*, in the form of loss of merit money, etc.

(c) *Suspension*, where the individual is not allowed to report for work for a specified period.

(d) *Dismissal*, which is the final sanction and which must be handled with the greatest care, to ensure that the organization's case can be upheld on appeal.

CHAPTER 9 | Legislation

We referred briefly in Chapter 1 to the *laissez-faire* philosophy. This was the belief that if everyone were encouraged to pursue his own advantage the greatest good for the greatest number would be achieved. Industry grew up in this background of thinking, and there is no doubt that the spirit of enterprise which it encouraged played a large part in our industrial development. Anyone with the initiative and drive to start a business found few obstacles in his way. If he pushed ahead and was successful, he made money—sometimes in very large quantities. These profits provided the capital for further developments, so new opportunities could be seized. The process gathered speed as it went along, and within 100 years or so it had changed our way of life in this country beyond recognition.

There is, however, another side to the picture, and not a very pretty one. Villagers had been pushed off the land by the enclosures which had broken up their little holdings. They crowded into the new industrial towns, which at that time were simply rows of cheap houses round the factories. There were few public services and no amenities. More people were seeking work than there were jobs going, so wages were low. For those who couldn't find work, the outlook was bleak indeed. There was only the workhouse, where conditions were deliberately made as unpleasant as possible to discourage people from relying on public assistance. This fitted in with the nineteenth-century philosophy, that it was only 'idleness and viciousness' that could prevent a man supporting himself. To avoid the workhouse, people would put up with almost anything. As a result of all this the worker in the factory was entirely at the mercy of his employer. And few employers of the time felt any need to show much consideration for those to whom they paid their wages.

Conditions in industry in the early nineteenth century were extremely bad. By present-day standards, in fact, they were shameful. Small children worked in the factories for long hours; women dragged tubs of coal in the mines on their hands and knees along the galleries; discipline was harsh and often brutally enforced. The 'dark Satanic mills' were a very real thing 150 years ago.

There were two means by which workers could have been protected from this state of affairs. One was the formation of trade unions, and the other was the passing of laws to lay down standards of employment. Unfortunately, neither of these was available at the time. Trade unions were illegal up till 1824, and even after this date there were many obstacles placed in the way of their development. Factory legislation was either non-existent or ineffective until 1833, partly because few people were interested in it, and partly because there were no means of enforcing it, or making sure that the laws were complied with in practice.

The first effective Factory Act was passed in 1833. This laid down that children under 9 could not be employed in the mills. Hours of work for children between 9 and 13 years of age were limited to 9 a day. Those between 13 and 18 years of age could work 12 hours a day. This may not appear exactly to guarantee an easy life to young people, but it did at least lay down a standard. And it provided for a staff of factory inspectors to ensure that this standard was enforced. Over the next few years the reports of these inspectors built up a picture of what was really going on in the early factories. This stirred up the public conscience and started a flow of legislation which continues to the present day.

This legislation lays down minimum conditions to which every employer must conform. If he fails to do so, legal proceedings can be taken against him. The factory inspectors are now part of the Department of Employment and Productivity which was originally set up as the Ministry of Labour at the end of the First World War. As with the Second World War, this caused the State to take a much larger part in the control of industry. These and other causes have led to the *laissez-faire* philosophy being greatly modified, if not abandoned altogether. We now take it for granted that limitations can be placed on the freedom of employers to lay down the conditions under which people will work. We also take it as natural that these conditions will be steadily improved. It is fair to say, however, that there have always been some employers who have provided conditions well above the statutory minimum. In fact, these employers have played a part, and are still playing a part, in raising the standards. Well over 100 years ago, Robert Owen's New Lanark Mills stood out among the squalor and degradation of the time as an example of what could be done.

The Factories Act, 1961

The minimum conditions for the present day were brought up to date in this Act. It contains five major sections:

1 *HEALTH*

Cleanliness must be maintained by the removal of dirt and refuse daily; weekly cleaning of floors; washing or whitewashing walls every 14 months; and painting every 7 years.

Overcrowding must be prevented by each person having 400 cubic feet of space, not counting anything more than 14 feet from the floor.

Temperature must be at least 60° Fahrenheit after the first hour where work is done sitting. There must be a thermometer which can be seen.

Ventilation must be secured by the circulation of fresh air, and workers must be protected against dust and fumes.

Lighting must be sufficient and *floors drained* where wet processes are carried on.

Sanitary accommodation must be provided to a certain standard for each sex separately and must be kept clean and adequately lighted.

Other matters dealt with under this heading are: eating in rooms where poisonous substances are used; underground rooms; lifting excessive weights; the employment of women and young persons where lead processes are used; and the notification of industrial poisoning or disease. Detailed regulations are laid down to ensure that adequate protection is given in such cases.

2 SAFETY

Accidents causing loss of life or more than 3 days' disablement must be reported to the District Inspector of Factories and entered in the General Register.

Fencing must be carried out to protect workers against moving machinery, pits, or vessels containing dangerous liquids.

Women or young persons must not clean machinery while it is moving.

Young persons must be trained and supervised before working on a dangerous machine.

Other matters dealt with under this section are: provision for cutting off power; proper guarding of new machines, inspection of hoists, lifts, chains, ropes, or lifting tackle every 6 months; examination of cranes every 14 months; sound construction of floors; safe means of access; precautions against gassing or explosions; examination of steam boilers and air receivers; and provision of goggles or screens where necessary. Each factory must have a certificate from the fire authority that means of escape are adequate; also fire alarms must be tested and reported on every 3 months.

3 *WELFARE*

This section deals with the provision of *drinking water*; *washing facilities* with hot and cold water, soap and towels; *accommodation* for hanging and drying *outdoor clothes*; facilities for *sitting* where work permits. In addition it lays down that *first-aid boxes* must be provided, and that where more than 150 persons are employed there must be an additional box for every further 150 people. A trained person must be in charge of each box.

4 *EMPLOYMENT OF WOMEN AND YOUNG PERSONS*

The general purpose of this section is to ensure that women and young persons under 18 years of age do not work more than 48 hours a week. Hours for young persons under 16 are limited to 44. There are, however, variations in how these hours can be worked. If the factory is on a 6-day week they can work between 7:00 a.m. and 8:00 p.m. (6:00 p.m. under 16) and between 7:00 a.m. and 1:00 p.m. on Saturday. They cannot work more than 9 hours (excluding intervals) on any one day, and not more than $4\frac{1}{2}$ hours without at least a $\frac{1}{2}$-hour break. If the factory is working a 5-day week, they can work a maximum of 10 hours a day. Sunday employment is prohibited and a minimum of holidays on Christmas, Good Friday, and Bank Holidays is laid down. Other provisions apply to shift working, and to van boys and others working outside the factory. Exceptions can be made to these regulations, however, provided that permission is given by the Employment Secretary or his representative. Young persons under 18 years of age must be examined by the appointed factory doctor and given a certificate of fitness to work.

5 *MISCELLANEOUS*

This section deals with outworkers, who must be listed on the prescribed form; piecework particulars, which must be supplied to the worker in writing; prohibition of deductions from wages; duties of persons employed not to endanger themselves or others; and giving notice 1 month before any premises are used as a factory. A General Register must be kept, while factory inspectors have wide powers of inspection to ensure that the Act is put into effect. Officers of local authorities and fire authorities have similar powers so far as their duties are concerned.

Readers of a book like this can only expect to have a general idea of the provisions of the Factories Act. More information can be gained from a short guide published by H.M. Stationery Office, or from the Act itself. In addition, there are regulations made by the Secretary under the Act which go into greater detail on certain matters. Dangerous trades, and certain types of machinery and processes, have their own regulations, and anyone specially concerned with these should make sure that he is familiar with the details.

Shops, Offices, and Railway Premises Act, 1963

A start was made at regulating conditions in the factories by the Act of 1833, and since then the standards have been steadily pushed upwards. It was not until 130 years later, however, that any regulations were applied to shops or offices. This situation has now been straightened out by the Shops, Offices, and Railway Premises Act of 1963. Generally speaking, it applies similar standards of health and safety to premises where people work, but which are not covered by the Factories Act. A general guide to this Act is available from H.M. Stationery Office.

Contracts of Employment Act, 1963

Every employee has a right to know the conditions under which he is working. This right has now been embodied in the Contracts of Employment Act, 1963. It lays a duty on employers to give their employees written information about their main terms of employment—pay, hours, holidays and holiday pay, sickness and sick pay, pensions and pension schemes, and notice. The object is to give employees a clear understanding of their rights and obligations under their contracts of employment. In addition to setting out these conditions in writing, this Act lays down minimum periods of notice. If an employee has been with the firm continuously for 26 weeks he is entitled to 1 week's notice. If he has been employed continuously for 2 years, he is entitled to 2 weeks' notice. And if he has been employed continuously for 5 years or more he is entitled to at least 4 weeks' notice. An employee, however, if he has been with his employer for 26 weeks or more, is only required to give 1 week's notice.

Redundancy Payments Act, 1965

Up to this point the line of development has been fairly clear—an attempt to ensure that working conditions shall be safe and decent, and that employees shall be protected from exploitation. From now on, however, we see an attempt to tackle different kinds of problem. One of these is the protection of employees from sudden changes in the demand for labour. Formerly, it was taken for granted that when a firm was short of orders, it would cut down its labour force. This might be justified on economic grounds—if there was no work it couldn't be expected to pay wages. But it meant that an employee might lose his job at any moment. And then what would he have to live on?

It is true that, from 1911 onwards, a National Insurance Scheme would provide some payment during unemployment. This also applied during sickness, while from 1908 old age pensions had helped to support people too old to work. As with everything else, the standards have crept up, until now the National Health Service ensures that no one goes short of adequate medical care. Until recently, however, these benefits did little more than provide for a subsistence or breadline level of existence. Now, however, benefits related to income help to prevent short periods of illness or unemployment bringing with them such a serious drop in the standard of living.

The sudden loss of a job nevertheless remains a nasty jolt to most people. And to cushion this shock, the Redundancy Payments Act became law in 1965. It defines redundancy as 'where the whole or main reason for an employee's dismissal is that his employer's need for employees to do work of a particular kind have diminished or ceased'. It makes no difference why the employer needs fewer employees—this may be, for example, because he is closing down, either altogether or in a particular area, or because of a trade recession, or because of a change in production arrangements. In all these cases, if the result is that the employer needs fewer employees, then those employees who have been dismissed have been dismissed because of redundancy.

Payments are arranged on the following scale for employees over 18 who have had 2 years' continuous service:

For each year of service between ages 18 and 21 inclusive—$\frac{1}{2}$ week's pay.
For each year of employment between ages 22 and 40 inclusive—1 week's pay.
For each year of service between ages 41 and 64 (59 for women) inclusive—$1\frac{1}{2}$ week's pay, up to a maximum of 20 years.

There are various provisos about the offer of other work to redundant employees, dismissal for reasons other than redundancy, etc., which we cannot go into here. Once again the details can be found in a guide to the Act which is available from H.M. Stationery Office. The scheme is financed by a fund to which employers make weekly contributions according to the number of men and women they employ. They may also claim a rebate from this fund when they make redundancy payments.

Disabled Persons (Employment) Act, 1944

A problem arose towards the end of the Second World War over the employment of people disabled through war wounds or other injuries. This was dealt with by requiring employers to take on a certain percentage (3%) of such people for jobs which were within their capacity. A corps of Disablement Rehabilitation Officers (DROs) was set up to advise on the employment of such people. Thus many who had suffered physical handicaps were enabled to earn a living.

Industrial Training Act, 1964

At this point the hard-headed business man might say: 'These measures are all very well for protecting the employee. But what does his employer get out of them? For that matter, what does the community get out of them? Are we turning our industry into a sort of charitable organization to keep people in jobs, look after them when they're sick, guard them against unemployment, and all the rest of it? The employer's got to meet competition if he's to stay in business. He's got other things to think about besides the welfare of his employees.' This is a fair point, and to keep the balance right we must take it into account.

The first answer, of course, is that many of these welfare services are financed on an insurance basis. Contributions from employees and the State, as well as those from the employer, offset the payments. So long as the fund is in balance, payments on behalf of the people in jobs cover the benefits received by those out of work. A second point may also be made which affects the standards of the community as a whole. If people are to work efficiently in modern industry, they must be looked after, or they must be able to look after themselves. The idea of a 'working class', which could be shunted round as labour was required, is completely out of date. It goes back to the early days of the Industrial Revolution, or even to the slave trade. And it is worth remembering that the most uneconomic type of labour is slave labour. If people have to live in squalor and poverty, they will never become the efficient operators which modern industry requires.

There is also a third point. Apart from setting minimum standards, these measures apply only in sickness and unemployment, or to women and young persons. There is no restriction on the hours of work for men. Nor, apart from certain trades where union organization was weak, has there been any limitation on the scope for bargaining over hours, wages, and other conditions through the trade unions.

The demands which the State makes on industry, therefore, do bring certain advantages to industry itself. They provide a 'floor' below which no one can fall. Employers cannot get away with offering conditions below this standard. Employees cannot fall into such distress that they are forced to accept such conditions. More and more people are rising above this 'floor', which is what everyone wants to see. Individual effort by employers and employed; collective bargaining through trade unions; the development of new methods and techniques; all these will play a part in raising our 'floor' to higher levels of self-respect and higher standards of living.

The next piece of legislation we must consider makes a positive contribution to raising standards of efficiency. It is thus a little different in nature from those which have been concerned with minimum standards. It may be the forerunner of others which make more positive demands on industry, but this we shall leave for the moment. The Industrial Training Act, 1964, sets out to raise the standards of training in industry by setting up Training Boards.

Under this Act each industry must have its own Industrial Training Board, financed by a levy. In the case of the Engineering Industry Training Board, this levy has initially been set at $2\frac{1}{2}\%$ of the payroll. After a study of the industry, these Boards set standards of training for the various levels of employee. If a firm, after inspection by the Board's staff, is meeting these standards, it receives a grant to cover its training expenses. It is possible for a firm to receive as much back in grant as it has paid in levy. In exceptional cases it can even receive more. This, of course, makes firms in the industry take their training more seriously.

We are still in the early stages of putting this Act into practice. Some Boards have been in existence longer than others and their plans are more advanced. Problems have to be faced in setting standards, providing instruction, and inspecting results. Small firms in particular have difficulties which are not met in the larger organizations where numbers of trainees justify internal arrangements. These and other problems are being dealt with, and the results will certainly be a raising of the standards of training at all grades, from operators through supervisors and specialists to management. The days when people learned their jobs by 'sitting next to Nellie' are numbered. As a result the industrial worker, supervisor, or manager will become a very different person.

Effects of Industrial Legislation
We have come a long way from the time when industry was left

to run itself without supervision from the State, or when the individual employee was left to fend for himself against his employer. Now, both in the longer-term issues and in day-to-day affairs, the State is setting standards which informed public opinion feels to be necessary. Let us consider the steps in this process as they would occur in an actual case—such as taking on a new employee to fill a vacancy.

1 The new employee might have been sent by the local Employment Exchange, now run by the Department of Employment and Productivity. These came into being (as Labour Exchanges) in 1909 to marry up vacancies with workers seeking employment. They now function as local offices of the Department and deal with unemployment and other benefits. Unemployed persons sign on at the Exchange and thus can be put forward for suitable vacancies notified by employers.

2 When accepted for employment, the starter's National Insurance cards must be collected from him. The firm is responsible for stamping these each week, the value of the stamps representing the employer's and employee's contribution. The Contracts of Employment Act requires that he be given the conditions under which he has to work in writing. If he is a young person under 18, he must be examined by the appointed factory doctor within 14 days.

3 When he starts, he must work under conditions laid down by the Factories Act. These cover not only the physical conditions of space, heating, lighting, etc., but also training and supervision if he has to work dangerous machinery.

4 If the firm wishes to qualify for a grant under the Industrial Training Act, it must train him up to the standards set by the appropriate Training Board.

(There is an area here which depends less on standards set by the State than on negotiation with the trade unions. This includes hours of work for adult men, wages, disputes, and appeals through representatives. The framework for this was set by various Acts of Parliament, but these fall under the heading of industrial relations, which is dealt with in detail in another volume of this series, *Industrial Relations in Supervisory Management* by A. W. Dickinson.)

5 Should the employee have an accident at work which involves more than 3 days' absence, this must be reported to the District Inspector of Factories. If the provisions of the Factories Act have not been kept, or if the special regulations which apply to the situation have been broken, the firm may be liable to prosecution.

6 Should the employee be off work through illness or injury, he

is entitled to medical treatment through the National Health Service, and to benefit through National Insurance.

7 Should he retire on reaching 65 or over, he is entitled to an old age pension.

8 Should his job become redundant, he is entitled to payment under the provisions of the Act.

These cover the State Regulations as they apply to the individual employee. There are, however, further demands made on the company.

9 Information, in the form of returns on various aspects of its activities, must be supplied to various Ministries.

10 Guidance and help is available on various future developments, e.g. the export trade.

11 If it wishes to expand, it may be prevented from doing so if it is already in an area of high employment, and encouraged by various inducements to open another establishment in an area where further employment opportunities are being sought—namely, in one of the Development Areas.

12 Still further demands may be made in the future, depending on how the economy develops. A Prices and Incomes Board was established as a means of control in the interests of the national economy. A Selective Employment Tax was introduced which made employees in service jobs more expensive than those in manufacturing employment. The National Economic Development Council (NEDC), which may be supplemented by regional or local bodies, is already taking a hand in guiding developments.

These activities may not affect the supervisory manager directly, but he should be aware of their longer-term implications. We are now one of a number of industrial nations, all competing for a share in world trade, and all trying to raise their internal levels of activity. Our survival depends on our ability to keep our place in this rat race. So there will be continual pressure to keep our industry up to date. This will mean changes—changes in organization, changes in technology, changes in products and methods of production. Both as individuals and as a nation, we must keep abreast of these changes if we are to survive.

SUMMARY

1 *What is the justification for factory legislation?*

Except in a situation of full employment, the worker is very much at the mercy of his employer. His only means of protection are collective bargaining through trade unions and State legislation laying down minimum standards. Since the first effective Factory Act of 1833, there has been a flow of legislation which has progressively raised these standards.

2 *What are the essential provisions of the current Factories Act?*

The Factories Act of 1961 lays down the present minimum standards. The main provisions are:

- (a) *Health*, covering cleanliness, overcrowding, temperature, ventilation, lighting, sanitary accommodation, etc.
- (b) *Safety*, dealing with the reporting of accidents, fencing of machinery, training of young persons before working dangerous machinery, etc.
- (c) *Welfare*, covering drinking-water, washing facilities, accommodation for outdoor clothes, seating, first-aid boxes.
- (d) *Employment of women and young persons under 18*, whose hours are limited to 48 a week and 44 for those under 16, with a maximum uninterrupted period of 4½ hours at any one time.
- (e) *Miscellaneous* provisions cover outworkers, piecework, etc., and also access by the factory inspector and keeping of a General Register in which medical examinations of young persons, etc., must be entered.

3 *Are minimum standards laid down for places other than factories?*

The Shops, Offices, and Railway Premises Act, 1963, lays down similar standards for other premises in which people may be employed.

4 *What is the intention behind the Contracts of Employment Act, 1963?*

To ensure that every employee knows the terms and conditions under which he is working before he accepts employment, this Act lays down that these must be given to him in writing. It also lays down minimum periods of notice, rising to 4 weeks after 5 years' service. The employee, however, need give only 1 week's notice.

5 *What is the intention behind the Redundancy Payments Act, 1965?*

To afford some protection to the employee's standard of living in the event of a sudden loss of employment, due to shortage of work, etc. This

Act provides for payments related to length of service, rising to $1\frac{1}{2}$ weeks' wages for each year between the ages of 41 and 64.

6 *What is the intention behind the Industrial Training Act, 1964?*

To raise the standards of training in British industry. This Act provides for Training Boards which are studying the training problems of each industry. In due course they will set up standards for different levels of job, survey the training facilities available, and carry out inspections in individual companies to see whether these standards are being met. The scheme is financed by levies on the firms in the industry, which can be paid back in grants, provided training arrangements are up to standard.

7 *What general tendencies are to be seen in legislation affecting industry?*

There has been a general movement away from a *laissez-faire* philosophy over the last 150 years. Much of the legislation has been aimed at protecting workers from exploitation by their employers and ensuring that their conditions of work are healthy, safe, and self-respecting. Recently, however, there has been a move towards raising standards of efficiency in training, while other moves have been directed towards making our industry more competitive in world markets. A further tendency can be seen towards making industry serve the community in providing employment by moving firms to areas of low economic activity. It seems likely that State guidance of industry will continue to increase, thus making the change more rapid.

When we think of the principles and practice of supervisory management, we must not tie ourselves down to any one company or any
one industry. We must stand back and look at the job in its own
right. We must think of the principles and practice as they apply to
any supervisory manager's job wherever it may be found. This means
disregarding the technical aspects of the job, for these will vary with
the firm or the industry. When we cut out the machines and process
and materials, what are we left with? We are left with people—with
men and women during the hours they spend at work. Thus the one
common factor which runs through every supervisory manager's job
is that he is in charge of people. And his success, in the last resort,
depends on how well he handles the human problems they present
to him.

This chapter is intended to serve as a general summing-up of the
principles and practice of supervisory management. It will thus deal
with the psychological aspects. And, for simplicity, it will be set out
in the form of questions and answers.

What is the essential task of the supervisory manager?

It is to draw out the effort of which people are capable and
channel it into the tasks which the organization requires of them.
People only put out effort when they think it is going to be rewarded.
The obvious reward they expect during working hours is money.
Thus, if the task is presented as a means of earning money, it will
automatically draw out a certain degree of effort. There are, however,
other forms of reward which people expect, even though they may
not be so obviously aware of them. These are the rewards of being
liked and accepted by other people, being taken seriously as individuals, and having a certain status and prestige. If the task offers
these rewards in addition to the wages it pays, it will call out
additional effort. If, however, the task offers only money and nothing
else, it will leave these expectations unsatisfied. There will thus be
spare capacity lying around during working hours. If this is not being
drawn into the activities of the organization, it will be attracted by
other activities. In some cases these may run counter to the purpose
of the organization. The supervisory manager, as the man immediately in charge, is the person most likely to be aware of this. Thus he,
and he alone, is in the position to ensure that the task is as satisfying

as possible to all aspects of the individual's personality, and thus to draw out the maximum reasonable effort from him during working hours.

Can we deal with people one at a time, as isolated individuals?

No. The individual's need to belong and to be appreciated makes him dependent on his relationships with others. These relationships will fall into patterns, where members of a group will be aware of each other as human beings, and will have formed expectations of how they will respond. Such groups will either be small and informal (primary groups), or large and impersonal (secondary groups). A role in a primary group will always be more satisfying than a role in a secondary group. Only in the primary group can one be an individual, liked and respected by the other members. The secondary group is a less satisfying experience, for it demands a formal, narrowly restricted role which gives little scope for self-expression as a person. To think of an organization as a formal, secondary group structure in which people are slotted like pegs into holes is to shut one's eyes to the day-by-day realities of working life.

How should we approach the problem of structure in an organization?

We should think of organization as a structure of groupings. If the roles in these groupings are fully satisfying to the individuals concerned, they will draw out the maximum reasonable effort during working hours. If these groupings are linked together by managers and supervisors who play dual, or connecting, roles, the structure will be properly integrated. It will form a unified framework through which purposes and objectives can be communicated downwards, and practical difficulties and problems communicated upwards. If, however, the formal chains of communication prove ineffective, groupings will tend to split off, and informal, unofficial methods of communication will come into being. This is a risk which is most noticeable at the lower levels in an organization. Here again, the supervisory manager is in the key position.

Can we simplify a modern organization into one chain of communication?

This is very difficult. For, in addition to the productive or line structure, we shall have the functional or specialist groupings. Each of these will have its own purpose, while the factory floor groupings will have their own patterns of relationships. We must, therefore, think of a fairly complex or pluralist structure, in which there will always be the danger of cross-purposes developing. There will thus be a heavy responsibility on those who act as connecting links to hold the structure together. This can be done by synthesizing the purposes of the component groups, or by achieving working compromises between them. As the person in direct touch with the factory floor groupings, which are furthest away from the centre of the organization, the supervisory manager perhaps carries the heaviest responsibility from this point of view.

What determines an individual's attitude to his work?

Attitudes are determined by the degree of total satisfaction which an individual derives from an activity. If he finds that his role during working hours, in addition to the wages he earns, gives him the rewards of belonging and being appreciated, his attitude to work will be a positive or favourable one. If, on the other hand, he feels that all he gets is his wages, without any feeling that he is taken seriously as an individual, then his attitude to work will be negative or hostile. In these circumstances, he will be drawn towards unofficial and possibly anti-management groupings. He will find the roles offered by these more satisfying, and his negative attitudes to the organization will be supplemented by positive attitudes to the groupings and activities which offer him protection from the organization. The individuals who take the leading roles in these anti-organizational groupings will acquire increasing influence at the lower levels. This is the process which leads to the disintegration of an organization. To counteract it, the supervisory manager must be kept in a position where he can be the focus of positive attitudes during working hours.

How do we reconcile the obvious differences between individuals with the demands we make on them at work?

Differences between individuals can be understood under five headings, for which scales based on a normal curve of distribution can be set up. These are:

Impact on others
Qualifications
Brains
Motivation
Adjustment

The same individual can be higher or lower on each of these different scales. The demands of jobs can also be expressed in terms of these scales. We should try to fit people into jobs where their personal qualities match up with these demands. Thus, the person of average motivation and adjustment will be satisfied in a fairly routine job, which demands little initiative and imposes no great stress. For a supervisory manager's job we need someone with more than average impact, good qualifications, and brains. We also need higher standards of drive and energy (motivation) and the ability to stand up to the stress of a responsible role (adjustment). Failure to match up people with jobs can lead to under-utilization of an individual's capacities, with consequent negative attitudes—or to placing people under more pressure than they can adjust to, with similar results.

Once we have placed an individual in a suitable job, can we then forget about him?

By no means. Day-to-day work is a constantly changing situation. Even the most routine job is carried out in a social group, where different kinds of pressure have to be met from time to time. The supervisory manager, besides himself adjusting to these pressures, has the task of helping others to cope with them. In the longer term, also, changing methods of production will make different demands on the individual. Skilled craft jobs give way to semi-skilled production jobs; while these in turn are replaced by technicians in charge of automated processes. Each of these changes will present a challenge to the individual, which he must either stand up to, or be overwhelmed by. Not only must the supervisory manager stand up to the challenges of his own changing role, he must help the people under him to adjust to the demands made upon them by new developments.

Is there any simple key to the understanding of other people?

This is very doubtful. Perhaps the most useful is the idea of the *self-image*, or the individual's own picture of the kind of person he is. This is neither logical nor very conscious, but it exerts a considerable influence on what a person will do willingly, because it accords with his self-image, and on what he will resent or rebel against, because it challenges his idea of himself. Most people think of themselves as responsible, adult human beings. Thus, if they are treated like ignorant, irresponsible children, they will react in a hostile or defensive manner. When this kind of reaction has been called out, they will be impossible to deal with unless severe disciplinary sanctions are applied. In present-day industry these are simply not available. The supervisory manager must thus handle his relationships at work in such a way that he does not call out this reaction. This has implications for his own image of the kind of person he is.

Can human attributes be measured?

Knowledge can be tested, either by the conventional examination or by questions requiring yes–no answers. These latter are considered to be more objective, since they do not depend on the individual's skill in written expression. This is a skill, nevertheless, which has considerable importance in working life. Brains can be estimated by means of intelligence tests. These set a series of small problems which do not depend on specialized knowledge, but which require the individual to spot relationships between words, figures, or diagrams. Performance is measured by relating the number of items done correctly against a normal curve of distribution based on the population as a whole. Special aptitudes can be estimated in a similar manner. Such tests and examinations come nearest to measurement in the assessment of human attributes. They deal, however, only with limited aspects of the total personality, i.e. qualifications and brains. It is very doubtful whether anything that could properly be called measurement can be applied to the other aspects—impact on others, motivation, and adjustment. In many cases these may be more important for success in a job. They can best be assessed, either by direct observation—impact on others—or by finding out what the individual has made of real-life situations in the past. This, if it can be suitably interpreted, shows his motivation and adjustment in action.

Can we look forward to an end to conflict in industry?

No. Not unless we want to see it go down the drain. Industry depends on drawing together groups of people with diverse and often conflicting interests. Customers want better value for money; investors want a higher return on their savings; employees want more wages and better conditions; the State wants a bigger income in taxation to provide more public services. These interests are all perfectly legitimate in themselves. Industry will only continue to function so long as it can find a series of working compromises between them. It can never hope to bring them into complete harmony. It is, in fact, the conflict between them that provides the dynamic to management. Anyone above the operator level must recognize this and must find his sense of achievement in getting results from handling the interactions of all these various interests. To hope for an end to conflict, with everyone working happily together in an atmosphere of mutual admiration, is not only unrealistic; it is to give up the struggle and start preparing for retirement on the old age pension.

Further Reading

Corder, G. G. *The Supervisor in the Mechanical Age*. Institute of Supervisory Management, Birmingham (1964).

Fraser, J. Munro. *Industrial Psychology*. Pergamon, Oxford (1962).

Fraser, J. Munro. *Employment Interviewing* (4th edition). Macdonald and Evans, London (1966).

Meade, J. P. de C. and F. W. Greig. *Supervisory Training*. H.M.S.O. (1966).

Seymour, W. Douglas. *Industrial Training for Manual Operations*. Pitman, London (1954).

Thurley, K. E. and A. C. Hamlin. *The Supervisor and His Job*. H.M.S.O. (1963).

White, J. R. H. *The Modern Supervisor*. Macdonald, London (1966).

Contracts of Employment Act, 1963. Revised Notes for Employers and Employees. H.M.S.O.

The Factories Act, 1961. A Short Guide. H.M.S.O.

A Guide to the Redundancy Payments Act, 1965. H.M.S.O.

The Offices, Shops and Railway Premises Act, 1963. A General Guide. H.M.S.O.

Index